2018 Supplement

Constitutional Law

Eighth Edition

Geoffrey R. Stone
Edward H. Levi Distinguished Service Professor of Law
University of Chicago Law School

Louis Michael Seidman
Carmack Waterhouse Professor of Constitutional Law
Georgetown University Law Center

Cass R. Sunstein
Robert Walmsley University Professor
Harvard Law School

Mark V. Tushnet
William Nelson Cromwell Professor of Law
Harvard Law School

Pamela S. Karlan
Kenneth & Harle Montgomery Professor of Public Interest Law
Stanford Law School

Wolters Kluwer

Published by Wolters Kluwer in New York.

Wolters Kluwer Legal & Regulatory U.S. serves customers worldwide with CCH, Aspen Publishers, and Kluwer Law International products. (www.WKLegaledu.com)

To contact Customer Service, e-mail customer.service@wolters kluwer.com, call 1-800-234-1660, fax 1-800-901-9075, or mail correspondence to:

Wolters Kluwer
Attn: Order Department
PO Box 990
Frederick, MD 21705

Printed in the United States of America.

1 2 3 4 5 6 7 8 9 0

ISBN 978-1-4548-9479-7

About Wolters Kluwer Legal & Regulatory U.S.

Wolters Kluwer Legal & Regulatory U.S. delivers expert content and solutions in the areas of law, corporate compliance, health compliance, reimbursement, and legal education. Its practical solutions help customers successfully navigate the demands of a changing environment to drive their daily activities, enhance decision quality and inspire confident outcomes.

Serving customers worldwide, its legal and regulatory portfolio includes products under the Aspen Publishers, CCH Incorporated, Kluwer Law International, ftwilliam.com and MediRegs names. They are regarded as exceptional and trusted resources for general legal and practice-specific knowledge, compliance and risk management, dynamic workflow solutions, and expert commentary.

Contents

Table of Cases

Italics indicate principal and intermediate cases.
All references are to page numbers in the main volume.

Table of Authorities

I
THE CONSTITUTION AND THE SUPREME COURT

E. *"Case or Controversy" Requirements and the Passive Virtues*

Page 114.   Before the Note, add the following:

GILL v. WHITFORD

138 S. Ct. 1916 (2018)

CHIEF JUSTICE ROBERTS delivered the opinion of the Court.

The State of Wisconsin, like most other States, entrusts to its legislature the periodic task of redrawing the boundaries of the State's legislative districts. A group of Wisconsin Democratic voters filed a complaint in the District Court, alleging that the legislature carried out this task with an eye to diminishing the ability of Wisconsin Democrats to convert Democratic votes into Democratic seats in the legislature. The plaintiffs asserted that, in so doing, the legislature had infringed their rights under the First and Fourteenth Amendments. . . .

[Certain] of the plaintiffs before us alleged that they had [a] personal stake in this case, but never followed up with the requisite proof. The District Court and this Court therefore lack the power to resolve their claims. We vacate the judgment and remand the case for further proceedings, in the course of which those plaintiffs may attempt to demonstrate standing in accord with the analysis in this opinion.

I

Wisconsin's Legislature consists of a State Assembly and a State Senate. The 99 members of the Assembly are chosen from single districts that must "consist of contiguous territory and be in as compact form as practicable." State senators are likewise chosen from single-member districts, which are laid on top of the State Assembly districts so that three Assembly districts form one Senate district.

The Wisconsin Constitution gives the legislature the responsibility to "apportion and district anew the members of the senate and assembly" at the first session following each census. In recent decades, however, that responsibility has just as often been taken up by federal courts. Following the census in 1980, 1990, and 2000, federal courts drew the State's legislative districts when the Legislature and the Governor — split on party lines — were unable to agree on new districting plans. The Legislature has broken the logjam just twice in the last 40 years. In 1983, a Democratic Legislature passed, and a Democratic Governor signed, a new districting plan that remained in effect until the 1990 census. In 2011, a Republican Legislature passed, and a Republican Governor signed, the districting plan at issue here, known as Act 43. Following the passage of Act 43, Republicans won majorities in the State Assembly in the 2012 and 2014 elections. In 2012, Republicans won 60 Assembly seats with 48.6% of the two-party statewide vote for Assembly candidates. In 2014, Republicans won 63 Assembly seats with 52% of the statewide vote.

In July 2015, twelve Wisconsin voters filed a complaint in the Western District of Wisconsin challenging Act 43. The plaintiffs identified themselves as "supporters of the public policies espoused by the Democratic Party and of Democratic Party candidates." They alleged that Act 43 is a partisan gerrymander that "unfairly favor[s] Republican voters and candidates," and that it does so by "cracking" and "packing" Democratic voters around Wisconsin.

As they explained:

> Cracking means dividing a party's supporters among multiple districts so that they fall short of a majority in each one. Packing means concentrating one party's backers in a few districts that they win by overwhelming margins.

Four of the plaintiffs—Mary Lynne Donohue, Wendy Sue Johnson, Janet Mitchell, and Jerome Wallace—alleged that they lived in State Assembly districts where Democrats have been cracked or packed. All of the plaintiffs also alleged that, regardless of "whether they themselves reside in a district that has been packed or cracked," they have been "harmed by the manipulation of district boundaries" because Democrats statewide "do not have the same opportunity provided to Republicans to elect representatives of their choice to the Assembly."

The plaintiffs argued that, on a statewide level, the degree to which packing and cracking has favored one party over another can be measured by a single calculation: an "efficiency gap" that compares each party's respective "wasted" votes across all legislative districts. "Wasted" votes are those cast for a losing candidate or for a winning candidate in excess of what that candidate needs to win. The plaintiffs alleged that Act 43 resulted in an unusually large efficiency gap that favored Republicans. . . .

Over the past five decades this Court has been repeatedly asked to decide what judicially enforceable limits, if any, the Constitution sets on the gerrymandering of voters along partisan lines. Our previous attempts at an answer have left few clear landmarks for addressing the question. What our precedents have to say on the topic is, however, instructive as to the myriad competing considerations that partisan gerrymandering claims involve. Our efforts to sort through those considerations have generated conflicting views both of how to conceive of the injury arising from partisan gerrymandering and of the appropriate role for the Federal Judiciary in remedying that injury. . . .

Our considerable efforts in [previous cases] leave unresolved whether such claims may be brought in cases involving allegations of partisan gerrymandering. In particular, two threshold questions remain: what is necessary to show standing in a case of this sort, and whether those claims are justiciable. Here we do not decide the latter question because the plaintiffs in this case have not shown standing under the theory upon which they based their claims for relief. . . .

We have long recognized that a person's right to vote is "individual and personal in nature." Thus, "voters who allege facts showing disadvantage to themselves as individuals have standing to sue" to remedy that disadvantage. The plaintiffs in this case alleged that they suffered such injury from partisan gerrymandering, which works through "packing" and "cracking" voters of one party to disadvantage those voters. That is, the plaintiffs claim a constitutional right not to be placed in legislative districts deliberately designed to "waste" their votes in elections where their chosen candidates will win in landslides (packing) or are destined to lose by closer margins (cracking).

To the extent the plaintiffs' alleged harm is the dilution of their votes, that injury is district specific. An individual voter in Wisconsin is placed in a single district. He votes for a single representative. [Its boundaries determine] whether and to what extent a particular voter is packed or cracked. This "disadvantage to [the voter] as [an] individual," therefore results from the boundaries of the particular district in which he resides. And a plaintiff's remedy must be "limited to the inadequacy that produced [his] injury in fact." In this case the remedy that is proper and sufficient lies in the revision of the boundaries of the individual's own district.

For similar reasons, we have held that a plaintiff who alleges that he is the object of a racial gerrymander — a drawing of district lines on the basis of race — has standing to assert only that his own district has been so gerrymandered. A plaintiff who complains of gerrymandering, but who does not live in a gerrymandered district, "assert[s] only a generalized grievance against governmental conduct of which he or she does not approve." Plaintiffs who complain of racial gerrymandering in their State cannot sue to invalidate the whole State's legislative districting map; such complaints must proceed "district-by-district." . . .

Here, the plaintiffs' partisan gerrymandering claims turn on allegations that their votes have been diluted. That harm arises from the particular composition of the voter's own district, which causes his vote — having been packed or cracked — to carry less weight than it would carry in another, hypothetical district. Remedying the individual voter's harm, therefore, does not necessarily require restructuring all of the State's legislative districts. It requires revising only such districts as are necessary to reshape the voter's district — so that the voter may be unpacked or uncracked, as the case may be. . . .

The plaintiffs argue that their legal injury is not limited to the injury that they have suffered as individual voters, but extends also to the statewide harm to their interest "in their collective representation in the legislature," and in influencing the legislature's overall "composition and policymaking." But our cases to date have not found that this presents an individual and personal injury of the kind required for Article III standing. On the facts of this case, the plaintiffs may not rely on "the kind of undifferentiated, generalized grievance about the conduct of government that we have refused to countenance in the past." A citizen's interest in the overall composition of the legislature is embodied in his right to vote for his representative. . . .

We leave for another day consideration of other possible theories of harm not presented here and whether those theories might present justiciable claims giving rise to statewide remedies. . . . The reasoning of this Court with respect to the disposition of this case is set forth in this opinion and none other. And the sum of the standing principles articulated here, as applied to this case, is that the harm asserted by the plaintiffs is best understood as arising from a burden on those plaintiffs' own votes. In this gerrymandering context that burden arises through a voter's placement in a "cracked" or "packed" district.

II

Four of the plaintiffs in this case—Mary Lynne Donohue, Wendy Sue Johnson, Janet Mitchell, and Jerome Wallace—pleaded a particularized burden along such lines. They alleged that Act 43 had "dilut[ed] the influence" of their votes as a result of packing or cracking in their legislative districts. The facts necessary to establish standing, however, must not only be alleged at the pleading stage, but also proved at trial. As the proceedings in the District Court progressed to trial, the plaintiffs failed to meaningfully pursue their allegations of individual harm. The plaintiffs did not seek to show such requisite harm since, on this record, it appears that not a single plaintiff sought to prove that he or she lives in a cracked or packed district. They instead rested their case at trial—and their arguments before this Court—on their theory of statewide injury to Wisconsin Democrats, in support of which they offered three kinds of evidence.

First, the plaintiffs presented the testimony of the lead plaintiff, Professor Whitford. But Whitford's testimony does not support any claim of packing or cracking of himself as a voter. Indeed, Whitford expressly acknowledged that Act 43 did not affect the weight of his vote. His testimony points merely to his hope of achieving a Democratic majority in the legislature—what the plaintiffs describe here as their shared interest in the composition of "the legislature as a whole." Under our cases to date, that is a collective political interest, not an individual legal interest, and the Court must be cautious that it does not become "a forum for generalized grievances."

Second, the plaintiffs provided evidence regarding the mapmakers' deliberations as they drew district lines. As the District Court recounted, the plaintiffs' evidence showed that the mapmakers "test[ed] the partisan makeup and performance of districts as they might be configured in different ways." Each of the mapmakers' alternative configurations came with a table that listed the number of "Safe" and "Lean" seats for each party, as well as "Swing" seats. The mapmakers also labeled certain districts as ones in which "GOP seats [would be] strengthened a lot," or which would result in "Statistical Pick Ups" for Republicans. And they identified still other districts in which "GOP seats [would be] strengthened a little," "weakened a little," or were "likely lost."

[That] evidence may well be pertinent with respect to any ultimate determination whether the plaintiffs may prevail in their claims against the defendants, assuming such claims present a justiciable controversy. But the question at this point is whether the plaintiffs have established injury in fact. That turns on effect, not intent, and requires a showing of a burden on the plaintiffs' votes that is "actual or imminent, not 'conjectural' or 'hypothetical.'"

Third, the plaintiffs offered evidence concerning the impact that Act 43 had in skewing Wisconsin's statewide political map in favor of Republicans. This evidence, which made up the heart of the plaintiffs' case, was derived from partisan-asymmetry studies. . . . The plaintiffs contend that these studies measure deviations from "partisan symmetry," which they describe as the "social scientific tenet that [districting] maps should treat parties symmetrically." In the District Court, the plaintiffs' case rested largely on a particular measure of partisan asymmetry—the "efficiency gap" of wasted votes. That measure was first developed in two academic articles published shortly before the initiation of this lawsuit. . . .

The plaintiffs and their *amici curiae* promise us that the efficiency gap and similar measures of partisan asymmetry will allow the federal courts—armed with just "a pencil and paper or a hand calculator"—to finally solve the problem of partisan gerrymandering that has confounded the Court for decades. We need not doubt the plaintiffs' math. The difficulty for standing purposes is that these calculations are an average measure. They do not address the effect that a gerrymander has on the votes of particular citizens. Partisan-asymmetry metrics such as the efficiency gap measure something else entirely: the effect that a gerrymander has on the fortunes of political parties.

Consider the situation of Professor Whitford, who lives in District 76, where, defendants contend, Democrats are "naturally" packed due to their geographic concentration, with that of plaintiff Mary Lynne Donohue, who lives in Assembly District 26 in Sheboygan, where Democrats like her have allegedly been deliberately cracked. By all accounts, Act 43 has not affected Whitford's individual vote for his Assembly representative — even plaintiffs' own demonstration map resulted in a virtually identical district for him. Donohue, on the other hand, alleges that Act 43 burdened her individual vote. Yet neither the efficiency gap nor the other measures of partisan asymmetry offered by the plaintiffs are capable of telling the difference between what Act 43 did to Whitford and what it did to Donohue. The single statewide measure of partisan advantage delivered by the efficiency gap treats Whitford and Donohue as indistinguishable, even though their individual situations are quite different.

That shortcoming confirms the fundamental problem with the plaintiffs' case as presented on this record. It is a case about group political interests, not individual legal rights. But this Court is not responsible for vindicating generalized partisan preferences. The Court's constitutionally prescribed role is to vindicate the individual rights of the people appearing before it.

In cases where a plaintiff fails to demonstrate Article III standing, we usually direct the dismissal of the plaintiff's claims. This is not the usual case. It concerns an unsettled kind of claim this Court has not agreed upon, the contours and justiciability of which are unresolved. Under the circumstances, and in light of the plaintiffs' allegations that Donohue, Johnson, Mitchell, and Wallace live in districts where Democrats like them have been packed or cracked, we decline to direct dismissal.

We therefore remand the case to the District Court so that the plaintiffs may have an opportunity to prove concrete and particularized injuries using evidence — unlike the bulk of the evidence presented thus far—that would tend to demonstrate a burden on their individual votes. We express no view on the merits of the plaintiffs' case. We caution, however, that "standing is not dispensed in gross": A plaintiff's remedy must be tailored to redress the plaintiff's particular injury.

The judgment of the District Court is vacated, and the case is remanded for further proceedings consistent with this opinion.

It is so ordered.

JUSTICE KAGAN, with whom JUSTICE GINSBURG, JUSTICE BREYER, and JUSTICE SOTOMAYOR join, concurring. . . .

I write to address in more detail what kind of evidence the present plaintiffs (or any additional ones) must offer to support that allegation. And I write to make some observations about what would happen if they succeed in proving standing—that is, about how their vote dilution case could then proceed on the merits. The key point is that the case could go forward in much the same way it did below: Given the charges of statewide packing and cracking, affecting a slew of districts and residents, the challengers could make use of statewide evidence and seek a statewide remedy.

I also write separately because I think the plaintiffs may have wanted to do more than present a vote dilution theory. Partisan gerrymandering no doubt burdens individual votes, but it also causes other harms. And at some points in this litigation, the plaintiffs complained of a different injury—an infringement of their First Amendment right of association. The Court rightly does not address that alternative argument: The plaintiffs did not advance it with sufficient clarity or concreteness to make it a real part of the case. But because on remand they may well develop the associational theory, I address the standing requirement that would then apply. As I'll explain, a plaintiff presenting such a theory would not need to show that her particular voting district was packed or cracked for standing purposes because that fact would bear no connection to her substantive claim. Indeed, everything about the litigation of that claim—from standing on down to remedy—would be statewide in nature.

Partisan gerrymandering, as this Court has recognized, is "incompatible with democratic principles." More effectively every day, that practice enables politicians to entrench themselves in power against the people's will. And only the courts can do anything to remedy the problem, because gerrymanders benefit those who control the political branches. None of those facts gives judges any excuse to disregard Article III's demands. The Court is right to say they were not met here. But partisan gerrymandering injures enough individuals and organizations in enough concrete ways to ensure that standing requirements, properly applied, will not often or long prevent courts from reaching the merits of cases like this one. Or from insisting, when they do, that partisan officials stop degrading the nation's democracy.

I . . .

The harm of vote dilution, as this Court has long stated, is "individual and personal in nature." It arises when an election practice—most commonly, the drawing of district lines—devalues one citizen's vote as compared to others. Of course, such practices invariably affect more than one citizen at a time. [But] we understood the injury as giving diminished weight to each particular vote, even if millions were so touched. In such cases, a voter living in an overpopulated district suffered "disadvantage to [herself] as [an] individual [ ]": Her vote counted for less than the votes of other citizens in her State. And that kind of disadvantage is what a plaintiff asserting a vote dilution claim—in the one-person, one-vote context or any other—always alleges.

To have standing to bring a partisan gerrymandering claim based on vote dilution, then, a plaintiff must prove that the value of her own vote has been "contract[ed]." And that entails showing, as the Court holds, that she lives in a district that has been either packed or cracked, for packing and cracking are the ways in which a partisan gerrymander dilutes votes. Consider the perfect form of each variety. When a voter resides in a packed district, her preferred candidate will win no matter what; when a voter lives in a cracked district, her chosen candidate stands no chance of prevailing. But either way, such a citizen's vote carries less weight—has less consequence—than it would under a neutrally drawn map. So when she shows that her district has been packed or cracked, she proves, as she must to establish standing, that she is "among the injured."

In many partisan gerrymandering cases, that threshold showing will not be hard to make. Among other ways of proving packing or cracking, a plaintiff could produce an alternative map (or set of alternative maps)—comparably consistent with traditional districting principles—under which her vote would carry more weight. For example, a Democratic plaintiff living in a 75%-Democratic district could prove she was packed by presenting a different map, drawn without a focus on partisan advantage, that would place her in a 60%-Democratic district. Or conversely, a Democratic plaintiff residing in a 35%-Democratic district could prove she was cracked by offering an alternative, neutrally drawn map putting her in a 50-50 district. The precise numbers are of no import. The point is that the plaintiff can show, through drawing alternative district lines, that partisan-based packing or cracking diluted her vote.

Here, the Court is right that the plaintiffs have so far failed to make such a showing. William Whitford was the only plaintiff to testify at trial about the alleged gerrymander's effects. He expressly acknowledged that his district would be materially identical under any conceivable map, whether or not drawn to achieve partisan advantage. That means Wisconsin's plan could not have diluted Whitford's own vote. . . . Four other plaintiffs differed from Whitford by alleging in the complaint that they lived in packed or cracked districts. But for whatever reason, they failed to back up those allegations with evidence as the suit proceeded. So they too did not show the injury—a less valuable vote—central to their vote dilution theory.

That problem, however, may be readily fixable. The Court properly remands this case to the District Court "so that the plaintiffs may have an opportunity" to "demonstrate a burden on their individual votes." That means the plaintiffs—both the four who initially made those assertions and any others (current or newly joined)—now can introduce evidence that their individual districts were packed or cracked. And if the plaintiffs' more general charges have a basis in fact, that evidence may well be at hand. Recall that the plaintiffs here alleged—and the District Court found—that a unified Republican government set out to ensure that Republicans would control as many State Assembly seats as possible over a decade (five consecutive election cycles). To that end, the government allegedly packed and cracked Democrats throughout the State, not just in a particular district or region. Assuming that is true, the plaintiffs should have a mass of packing and cracking proof, which they can now also present in district-by-district form to support their standing. In other words, a plaintiff residing in each affected district can show, through an alternative map or other evidence, that packing or cracking indeed occurred there. And if (or to the extent) that test is met, the court can proceed to decide all distinctive merits issues and award appropriate remedies.

When the court addresses those merits questions, it can consider statewide (as well as local) evidence. Of course, the court below and others like it are currently debating, without guidance from this Court, what elements make up a vote dilution claim in the partisan gerrymandering context. But assume that the plaintiffs must prove illicit partisan intent—a purpose to dilute Democrats' votes in drawing district lines. The plaintiffs could then offer evidence about the mapmakers' goals in formulating the entire statewide map (which would predictably carry down to individual districting decisions). So, for example, the plaintiffs here introduced proof that the mapmakers looked to partisan voting data when drawing districts throughout the State—and that they graded draft maps according to the amount of advantage those maps conferred on Republicans. . . .

Similarly, cases like this one might warrant a statewide remedy. Suppose that mapmakers pack or crack a critical mass of State

Assembly districts all across the State to elect as many Republican politicians as possible. And suppose plaintiffs residing in those districts prevail in a suit challenging that gerrymander on a vote dilution theory. The plaintiffs might then receive exactly the relief sought in this case. [The] Court recognizes as much. It states that a proper remedy in a vote dilution case "does not *necessarily* require restructuring all of the State's legislative districts." Not necessarily — but possibly. It all depends on how much redistricting is needed to cure all the packing and cracking that the mapmakers have done.

II

Everything said so far relates only to suits alleging that a partisan gerrymander dilutes individual votes. [But] partisan gerrymanders inflict other kinds of constitutional harm as well. Among those injuries, partisan gerrymanders may infringe the First Amendment rights of association held by parties, other political organizations, and their members. The plaintiffs here have sometimes pointed to that kind of harm. To the extent they meant to do so, and choose to do so on remand, their associational claim would occasion a different standing inquiry than the one in the Court's opinion. . . .

Standing, we have long held, "turns on the nature and source of the claim asserted." Indeed, that idea lies at the root of today's opinion. It is because the Court views the harm alleged as vote dilution that it (rightly) insists that each plaintiff show packing or cracking in her own district to establish her standing. But when the harm alleged is not district specific, the proof needed for standing should not be district specific either. And the associational injury flowing from a statewide partisan gerrymander, whether alleged by a party member or the party itself, has nothing to do with the packing or cracking of any single district's lines. The complaint in such a case is instead that the gerrymander has burdened the ability of like-minded people across the State to affiliate in a political party and carry out that organization's activities and objects.

Because a plaintiff can have that complaint without living in a packed or cracked district, she need not show what the Court demands today for a vote dilution claim. Or said otherwise: Because on this alternative theory, the valued association and the injury to it are statewide, so too is the relevant standing requirement.

On occasion, the plaintiffs here have indicated that they have an associational claim in mind. In addition to repeatedly alleging vote dilution, their complaint asserted in general terms that Wisconsin's districting plan infringes their "First Amendment right to freely associate with each other without discrimination by the State based on that association." Similarly, the plaintiffs noted before this Court that "[b]eyond diluting votes, partisan gerrymandering offends First Amendment values by penalizing citizens because of . . . their association with a political party." And finally, the plaintiffs' evidence of partisan asymmetry well fits a suit alleging associational injury. . . .

In the end, though, I think the plaintiffs did not sufficiently advance a First Amendment associational theory to avoid the Court's holding on standing. Despite referring to that theory in their complaint, the plaintiffs tried this case as though it were about vote dilution alone. . . .

But nothing in the Court's opinion prevents the plaintiffs on remand from pursuing an associational claim, or from satisfying the different standing requirement that theory would entail. [Nothing] about that injury is "generalized" or "abstract," as the Court says is true of the plaintiffs' dissatisfaction with the "overall composition of the legislature." A suit raising an associational theory complains of concrete "burdens on a disfavored party" and its members as they pursue their political interests and goals. And when the suit alleges that a gerrymander has imposed those burdens on a statewide basis, then its litigation should be statewide too — as to standing, liability, and remedy alike. . . .

[An opinion by Justice Thomas, joined by Justice Gorsuch, concurring in part and concurring in the judgment has been omitted.]

Page 118.   Before section b of the Note, add the following:

In Trump v. Hawaii, 138 S. Ct. 2392 (2018), the Court upheld a presidential proclamation that imposed a "travel ban" on nationals from certain countries. (The case is discussed in greater detail in the supplement to page 1487 of the Main Volume). Before resolving the merits, the Court explored the question of standing. It bracketed the question whether plaintiffs might have standing on the ground that the proclamation violated their right to be free from federal establishments of religion. Instead it noted that the "three individual plaintiffs assert another, more concrete injury: the alleged real-world effect that the Proclamation has had in keeping them separated from certain relatives who seek to enter the country." The Court agreed "that a person's interest in being united with his relatives is sufficiently concrete and particularized to form the basis of an Article III injury in fact."

II

FEDERALISM AT WORK: CONGRESS AND THE NATIONAL ECONOMY

D. State Regulation of Interstate Commerce

Page 296.   At the end of the Note, add the following:

The Court overruled *Quill* in South Dakota v. Wayfair, Inc., ___ S. Ct. ___ (2018). South Dakota had attempted to impose its sales tax on large internet retailers who had no physical presence in the state but shipped substantial amounts of goods into it. (Formally, local purchasers are supposed to pay a use tax themselves, but, according to the Court, "compliance rates are notoriously low.") "Each year," Justice Kennedy's opinion for the majority observed, "the physical presence rule becomes further removed from economic reality and results in significant revenue losses to the States." The Court therefore held that the rule that a state can tax only activities with a "substantial nexus" to it did not require that the retailer have a physical presence in the state. It was clear that the retailer had sufficient "economic and virtual contacts" with South Dakota to satisfy the general "substantial nexus" requirement. The state sought to impose its taxes only on sellers who did more than $100,000 worth of business in the state. "This quantity of business could not have occurred unless the seller availed itself of the substantial privilege of carrying on business in South Dakota. And [Wayfair and other sellers] are large, national companies that undoubtedly maintain an extensive virtual presence."

On the question of Congress's role, Chief Justice Roberts, dissenting (joined by Justices Breyer, Sotomayor, and Kagan), wrote that, though he agreed that *Quill* was "wrongly decided," "[any] alteration of [the] rules with the potential to disrupt the development of [a] critical segment of the economy should be undertaken by Congress." He noted that "Congress has been considering whether to alter the rule established in *Bellas Hess* for some time. [By] suddenly changing the ground rules, the Court may have waylaid Congress's consideration of the issue. [State] officials can be expected to redirect their attention from working with Congress on a national solution." Observing that "[over] 10,000 jurisdictions levy sales taxes," with different rates, exemptions, and product category definitions, the Chief Justice argued that compliance with these varying rules would impose large costs, particularly on small businesses. "People starting a business selling their embroidered pillowcases or carved decoys can offer their wares throughout the country—but probably not if they have to figure out the tax due on every sale." (Might the requirement of a "substantial nexus" protect such businesses?) For the Chief Justice, "A good reason to leave these matters to Congress is that legislators may more directly consider the competing interests at stake. [Congress] might elect to accommodate these competing interests, by, for example, allowing States to tax Internet sales by remote retailers only if revenue from such sales exceeds some set amount per year."

Justice Kennedy responded, "While it can be conceded that Congress has the authority to change the physical presence rule, Congress cannot change the constitutional default rule. It is inconsistent with the Court's proper role to ask Congress to address a false constitutional premise of this Court's own creation."

Note that the "constitutional default rule" allocates the burden of securing congressional action. The "physical presence" rule allocates that burden to the states, who must secure congressional legislation authorizing them to tax retailers who lack a physical presence. Despite efforts such as those described by the Chief Justice, the states had been unable to secure such legislation over several decades of effort. *Wayfair* allocates the burden to internet retailers, who must (if they want) secure legislation setting national standards for taxation of their sales. The Chief Justice observed that states collected between 87 and 96 percent of the sales taxes associated with sales by the 100 largest internet retailers, and that "[some] companies, including the online behemoth Amazon, now voluntarily collect and remit sales tax in every State that assesses one—even those in which they have no physical presence." Should these considerations affect the Court's choice of default rule (and if so, how)?

III

THE SCOPE OF CONGRESS'S POWERS: TAXING AND SPENDING, WAR POWERS, INDIVIDUAL RIGHTS, AND STATE AUTONOMY

D. The Tenth Amendment as a Federalism-Based Limitation on Congressional Power

Page 369. At the end of section 2 of the Note, add the following:

2a. *What counts as commandeering?* In *New York*, the Supreme Court dealt with a federal statute that essentially required states to enact legislation. Can federal statutes that prohibit states from enacting legislation violate the anticommandeering principle? In this light, consider Murphy v. National Collegiate Athletic Ass'n, 138 S. Ct. 1461 (2018).

In 1992, Congress enacted the Professional and Amateur Sports Protection Act (PASPA). PASPA did not make sports betting a violation of federal law, but it did prohibit states from "authoriz[ing]" betting on sporting events.

At the time PASPA was enacted, New Jersey prohibited betting on sports, but the state enacted legislation that would have legalized sports betting in Atlantic City and at horseracing tracks. When the NCAA and three major professional sports leagues brought an action to enjoin New Jersey's sports betting law, New Jersey responded that PASPA violated the anticommandeering principle because it prevented the State from modifying or repealing its laws prohibiting sports gambling.

In an opinion by Justice Alito, the Supreme Court agreed. The Court declared that the repeal of existing laws banning gambling was an "authoriz[ation]" of gambling. PASPA's provision forbidding states from authorizing sports gambling "violates the anticommandeering rule. That provision unequivocally dictates what a state legislature may and may not do. . . . [S]tate legislatures are put under the direct control of Congress. It is as if federal officers were installed in state legislative chambers and were armed with the authority to stop legislators from voting on any offending proposals. A more direct affront to state sovereignty is not easy to imagine." PASPA's defenders had argued that commandeering occurs only when Congress commands a state or local government to do something, and not when Congress prohibits them from acting. The Court disagreed: "This distinction is empty. It was a matter of happenstance that the laws challenged in *New York* and *Printz* commanded 'affirmative' action as opposed to imposing a prohibition. The basic principle—that Congress cannot issue direct orders to state legislatures—applies in either event.

"Here is an illustration. PASPA includes an exemption for States that permitted sports betting at the time of enactment, . . . but suppose Congress did not adopt such an exemption. Suppose Congress ordered States with legalized sports betting to take the affirmative step of criminalizing that activity and ordered the remaining States to retain their laws prohibiting sports betting. There is no good reason why the former would intrude more deeply on state sovereignty than the latter."

Is the action/inaction distinction really meaningless with respect to commandeering? Does Murphy significantly expand the doctrine?

IV
THE DISTRIBUTION OF NATIONAL POWERS

A. Introduction

Page 379. At the end of section 2 of the Note, add the following:

Many modern critics of separation of powers claim that Madison's theory has not worked as he intended because he failed to anticipate the growth of political parties. Today, these critics claim, politicians are loyal to their fellow party members rather than to the branch where they sit.

Compare Fontana and Huq, Institutional Loyalties in Constitutional Law, 85 U. Chi. L. Rev. 1, 10, 11 (2018). The authors argue that "[The] behavior of federal officials cannot always be explained simply by partisan or ideological motives. The current working of our constitutional system evinces the lingering influence of institutional loyalty of the kind Madison anticipated, particularly in the executive and judicial contexts."

As a normative matter, they claim that institutional loyalties are not "intrinsically desirable ends," but instead should be valued only when they "motivate constitutional compliance, counteract disabling partisan polarization, and dampen the agency costs of representative democracy."

Applying these criteria, they conclude that it would be desirable to "[increase] institutional loyalty within the legislature while diminishing it within the judiciary. The executive branch presents a subtler question. In some contexts, the executive is powerfully motivated by institutional loyalty in ways that redound to the public good. This may be especially so when elected actors press agendas that are directly disruptive of longstanding democratic or institutional practice. But in other regards, there is a case for diluting their effects in ways that protect the rule of law from potentially corrupting and distorting influences."

B.   Case Study: Presidential Seizure

Page 391.   After subsection c of the Note, add the following:

c1. "As a logical matter, the notion that discretion increases as sources increase is incorrect without more. Sometimes the opposite is true. Indeed adding sources tends to drive down the probability that all sources will cancel out into uncertainty and yield discretion, according to a simple model of interpretation. . . .

"As an empirical matter, the effect of additional sources seems equally contingent. . . .

"[Analyzing] a new set of appellate decisions casts doubt on an earlier finding that increasing the stock of precedents ultimately increases judicial discretion. [New] data from appellate briefs reinforces an earlier finding that increasing brief length can reduce judicial preferences for affirmance; but the new data also indicate that more issues may increase affirmance rates, and the data fail to show a relationship between the number of sources cited and affirmance. [An] expanded set of district court decisions supports an earlier finding that a large number of doctrinal factors may prompt judges to prioritize law's core factors, without evidence of conventional ideological influence. But the data do not show that more spinning takes place when judges are asked to consider more factors. If anything, the opposite might be true." Samaha, Looking over a Crowd—Do More Interpretive Sources Mean More Discretion?, 92 N.Y.U. L. Rev. 554, 558-60 (2017).

C.   Foreign Affairs

Page 410.   Before the Note, add the following:

Note: The Status of Individual Rights in the National Security Context.

In her plurality opinion in *Hamdi*, Justice O'Connor asserts that even in times of armed conflict, the Court should "not give short shrift to the values that the country holds dear," and that "a state of war is not a blank check for the President when it comes to the rights of the Nation's citizens."

Compare Trump v. Hawaii, 138 S. Ct. 2392 (2018), where the Court rejected an establishment clause claim relating to a presidential order placing entry restrictions on nationals of eight foreign states, six of which were predominantly Muslim. (The opinion is considered at greater length in the supplement to page 1487 of the Main Volume). The order came in the context of repeated statements by President Trump, which the plaintiffs alleged revealed anti-Muslim bias. The plaintiffs claimed that under ordinary establishment clause principles, this bias was sufficient to make the order unconstitutional, but the Court, in an opinion by Justice Roberts, declined to follow these principles in the context of presidential decisions regarding national security and entry of foreign nationals into the country.

The Court cited prior cases holding that the admission and exclusion of foreign nationals is a "fundamental sovereign attribute exercised by the Government's political departments largely immune from judicial control" and that even when entry decisions affected the constitutional rights of American citizens, it had "limited [its] review to whether the Executive gave a 'facially legitimate and bona fide' reason for its action." According to the Court,

> [a] conventional application of [these principles], asking only whether the policy is facially legitimate and bona fide, would put an end to our review. But the Government has suggested that it may be appropriate here for the inquiry to extend beyond the facial neutrality of the order. For our purposes today, we assume that we may look behind the face of the Proclamation to the extent of applying rational basis review. That standard of review considers whether the entry policy is plausibly related to the Government's stated objective to protect the country and improve vetting processes.

Applying this standard, the Court found that there was a rational basis for the order and that it was therefore constitutionally permissible.

Can Trump v. Hawaii be reconciled with *Hamdi?*

In Korematsu v. United States, the Court upheld the constitutionality of a presidential order issued pursuant to the President's war power excluding Japanese-American citizens from certain parts of the United States. (*Korematsu* is discussed at page 532 of the Main Volume.) It did so, however, only after determining that the order satisfied strict scrutiny. Is the Court's use of rational basis review in Trump v. Hawaii consistent with *Korematsu?* Responding to Justice Sotomayor's invocation of *Korematsu* in her dissenting opinion, the Court wrote the following:

> *Korematsu* has nothing to do with this case. The forcible relocation of U.S. citizens to concentration camps, solely and explicitly on the basis of race, is objectively unlawful and outside the scope of Presidential authority. But it is wholly inapt to liken that morally repugnant order to a facially neutral policy denying certain foreign nationals the privilege of admission. The entry suspension is an act

that is well within executive authority and could have been taken by any other President—the only question is evaluating the actions of this particular President in promulgating an otherwise valid Proclamation. The dissent's reference to *Korematsu*, however, affords this Court the opportunity to make express what is already obvious: *Korematsu* was gravely wrong the day it was decided, has been overruled in the court of history, and—to be clear—"has no place in law under the Constitution."

Page 420.   After the first paragraph of section 2 of the Note, add the following:

As pointed out in Bradley and Goldsmith, Presidential Control over International Law, 131 Harv. L. Rev. 1201, 1210 (2018), executive agreements have become the dominant mode of United States agreement-making. Between 1990 and 2012, the United States entered 5,491 executive agreements, but only 366 treaties.

Is the growing use of the executive agreement technique constitutionally troubling? Most commentators agree that it is not if the President is acting pursuant to a congressional delegation or pursuant to relatively clear Article II authority such as the President's power to recognize foreign governments. Suppose, though, that there is neither a clear delegation nor a clear source of Article II authority? Consider in this regard the implications of Dames & Moore v. Regan, page 394 of the Main Volume, where the Court upheld the agreement ending the Iran Hostage Crisis by interpreting prior congressional silence as acquiescence. Compare Koh, Triptych's End: A Better Framework To Evaluate 21st Century International Lawmaking, 121 Yale On Line Law Journal (2017) (*"Dames & Moore* seems to have recognized a modern truth: that Congress cannot and does not pass judgment on each and every act undertaken by the Executive that has external effects.") with Bradley and Goldsmith, supra, at 1262 ("The considerations that were important [in *Dames & Moore*]—historical practice and independent presidential authority—do not hold for executive regulation of many other subjects, such as intellectual property or the environment.")

D.   *Domestic Affairs*

Page 445.   At the end of section 1 of the Note, add the following:

Consider the extent to which these cases, and the cases discussed in the remainder of this chapter, reflect a broader, unresolved controversy over the constitutionality of a modern "administrative state" that vests broad lawmaking power in agencies that have both adjudicative and rulemaking authority. See, e.g., P. Hamburger, The Administrative Threat 22 (2017):

> The Constitution establishes only regular avenues of power, and thereby blocks irregular or extralegal power. To be precise, it blocks extralegal lawmaking by placing legislative power exclusively in Congress, and it prevents extralegal adjudication by placing judicial power exclusively in the courts.
> It thus authorizes only two pathways for governments to bind Americans, in the sense of imposing legal obligation on them. [These] are [the government's] lawful options. Other attempts to bind Americans, whether with rules or adjudications, are unconstitutional.

Compare Metzger, 1930s Redux: The Administrative State Under Siege, 131 Harv. L. Rev. 1, 7 (2017):

> [The] administrative state is essential for actualizing constitutional separation of powers today, serving both to constrain executive power and to mitigate the dangers of

presidential unilateralism while also enabling effective governance. [Anti-administrativists] fail to recognize that the key administrative state features that they condemn, such as bureaucracy with its internal oversight mechanisms and expert civil service, are essential for the accountable, constrained, and effective exercise of executive power.

Page 448.   Before section 5 of the Note, add the following:

Compare Lucia v. Securities and Exchange Comm'n, ___ S. Ct. ___ (2018). The Securities and Exchange Commission delegates many administrative proceedings to administrative law judges (ALJs), who are appointed by SEC staff members, rather than by the Commission itself. The ALJs hear enforcement actions and exercise authority comparable to that of a federal district judge conducting a bench trial. At the conclusion of hearings, the ALJs issue "initial decisions" setting out findings regarding material facts and appropriate relief. The Commission can review ALJ decisions, but if it opts against review, the decisions are final and are deemed the action of the Commission.

In a 6-3 decision, the Court, per Justice Kagan, held that ALJs were "Officers of the United States" and therefore had to be appointed by the President, courts of law, or heads of department. Because staff members of the Commission fit into none of these categories, the appointments were unconstitutional.

Relying on its earlier decision in Freytag v. Commissioner, 501 U.S. 868 (1991), the Court held that ALJs were "Officers" because they held "a continuing office," and exercised "significant discretion" when carrying out "important functions." The Court relied on the fact that ALJs "critically shape the administrative record" and have the authority to issue final decisions.

Justice Thomas, joined by Justice Gorsuch, wrote a concurring opinion. Justice Breyer, joined by Justice Ginsburg and, in part, by

Justice Sotomayor, concurred in the judgment in part and dissented in part. Justice Sotomayor, joined by Justice Ginsburg, dissented.

In Ortiz v. United States, ___ S. Ct. ___ (2018), the Court held that the appointments clause posed no obstacle to an individual serving as an inferior officer on one Article I court while simultaneously serving as a principal officer on another Article I court.

Page 460. Before section 5 of the Note, add the following:

In Lucia v. Securities and Exchange Comm'n, ___ S. Ct. ___ (2018), the Court held that administrative law judges (ALJs) who adjudicated disputes relating to securities laws were "Officers of the United States." (The case is discussed at the supplement to page 448 of the Main Text). Given this holding, does the "double insulation" doctrine mean that statutory restrictions on the removal of ALJs are unconstitutional? In *Lucia*, the Court declined to address this issue. Compare Justice Breyer's opinion concurring in the judgment in part and dissenting in part:

> *If* the *Free Enterprise Fund* Court's holding applies equally to the administrative law judges — and I stress the "if" — then to hold that the administrative law judges are "Officers of the United States" is *perhaps*, to hold that their removal protections are unconstitutional. This would risk transforming administrative law judges from independent adjudicators into *dependent* decisionmakers, serving at the pleasure of the Commission. Similarly, to apply *Free Enterprise Fund*'s holding to high-level civil servants threatens to change the nature of our merit-based civil service as it has existed from the time of President Chester Alan Arthur.

Justice Breyer pointed to two possible grounds for distinguishing ALJs from the Board members discussed in *Free Enterprise*

Fund. First, ALJs "perform adjudicative rather than enforcement or policymaking functions." Second, the kind of "for cause" protection provided for Board members was "unusually high" and more significant than the protection enjoyed by ALJs. Is either of these differences sufficient to distinguish between the two situations?

V
EQUALITY AND THE CONSTITUTION

C. Equal Protection Methodology: Heightened Scrutiny and the Problem of Race

Page 540. **Before the Note, and at the end of section 2 of the prior Note, add the following:**

In Trump v. Hawaii, 138 S. Ct. 2392 (2018), the Supreme Court upheld a presidential proclamation that placed entry restrictions on foreign nationals from several countries. (The proclamation was commonly referred to as a "travel ban.") (The case is discussed at greater length in the supplement to page 1487 of the Main Volume.)

Challengers, including the state of Hawaii, sued. They alleged, among other things, that the proclamation violated the Constitution because it targeted Muslims, in contravention of the establishment clause of the First Amendment.

In an opinion by Chief Justice Roberts, the Court rejected the argument that heightened scrutiny should apply to the proclamation because it had been "issued for the unconstitutional purpose of excluding Muslims." Instead, the Court applied rational basis review, although it "assume[d] that we may look behind the face of the Proclamation to the extent of applying rational basis review. That standard of review considers whether the entry policy is plausibly related to the Government's stated objective to protect the country and improve vetting processes. As a result, we may consider plaintiffs' extrinsic evidence, but will uphold the policy so long as it can reasonably be understood to result from a justification independent of unconstitutional grounds."

In the course of upholding the ban, the majority rejected the dissent's assertion that there were "stark parallels" between the internment policy at issue in *Korematsu* and the travel ban:

> Finally, the dissent invokes Korematsu v. United States . . . . Whatever rhetorical advantage the dissent may see in doing so, *Korematsu* has nothing to do with this case. The forcible relocation of U.S. citizens to concentration camps, solely and explicitly on the basis of race, is objectively unlawful and outside the scope of Presidential authority. But it is wholly inapt to liken that morally repugnant order to a facially neutral policy denying certain foreign nationals the privilege of admission. The entry suspension is an act that is well within executive authority and could have been taken by any other President—the only question is evaluating the actions of this particular President in promulgating an otherwise valid Proclamation.
>
> The dissent's reference to *Korematsu*, however, affords this Court the opportunity to make express what is already obvious: *Korematsu* was gravely wrong the day it was decided, has been overruled in the court of history, and—to be clear—"has no place in law under the Constitution." 323 U.S., at 248 (Jackson, J., dissenting).

Page 557.   At the end of section 4 of the Note, add the following:

In Abbott v. Perez, 138 S. Ct. ___ (2018), the Court addressed the legality of several congressional and state legislative districts drawn in Texas after the 2010 census. The districts were originally drawn by the state legislature in 2011, but because that plan was immediately challenged in court, it never officially went into effect. Instead, the districts were put into effect by being included in an interim judicial remedy. They were then reenacted unchanged by the legislature in 2013.

The Court, in an opinion by Justice Alito, rejected the challengers' claim that the districts had been drawn for the purpose of diluting the voting strength of racial minorities. The Court gave little weight to the district court's finding that the plan was tainted by the discriminatory motivations of legislators in 2011:

> The allocation of the burden of proof and the presumption of legislative good faith are not changed by a finding of past discrimination. "[P]ast discrimination cannot, in the manner of original sin, condemn governmental action that is not itself unlawful." The "ultimate question remains whether a discriminatory intent has been proved in a given case." . . . But we have never suggested that past discrimination flips the evidentiary burden on its head.

The Court distinguished *Hunter* as addressing "a very different situation":

> *Hunter* involved an equal protection challenge to an article of the Alabama Constitution adopted in 1901 at a constitutional convention avowedly dedicated to the establishment of white supremacy. The article disenfranchised anyone convicted of any crime on a long list that included many minor offenses. The court below found that the article had

been adopted with discriminatory intent, and this Court accepted that conclusion. The article was never repealed, but over the years, the list of disqualifying offenses had been pruned, and the State argued that what remained was facially constitutional. This Court rejected that argument because the amendments did not alter the intent with which the article, including the parts that remained, had been adopted. But the Court specifically declined to address the question whether the then-existing version would have been valid if "[re]enacted today."

In these cases, we do not confront a situation like the one in *Hunter*. Nor is this a case in which a law originally enacted with discriminatory intent is later reenacted by a different legislature. The 2013 Texas Legislature did not reenact the plan previously passed by its 2011 predecessor. Nor did it use criteria that arguably carried forward the effects of any discriminatory intent on the part of the 2011 Legislature. Instead, it enacted, with only very small changes, plans that had been developed by the Texas court . . . .

Instead of holding the plaintiffs to their burden of overcoming the presumption of good faith and proving discriminatory intent, [the district court] reversed the burden of proof. It imposed on the State the obligation of proving that the 2013 Legislature had experienced a true "change of heart" and had "engage[d] in a deliberative process to ensure that the 2013 plans cured any taint from the 2011 plans." . . .

In holding that the District Court disregarded the presumption of legislative good faith and improperly reversed the burden of proof, we do not suggest either that the intent of the 2011 Legislature is irrelevant or that the plans enacted in 2013 are unassailable because they were previously adopted on an interim basis by the Texas court. Rather, both the intent of the 2011 Legislature and the court's adoption of the interim plans are relevant to the extent that they naturally give rise to—or tend to refute—inferences regarding the intent of the 2013 Legislature. They must be weighed together with any other direct and circumstantial evidence of that Legislature's intent. But when all the relevant evidence in the record is taken into account, it is plainly insufficient to prove that the 2013 Legislature acted in bad faith and engaged in intentional discrimination.

Page 609.   At the end of section 3 of the Note, add the following:

Compare the treatment of standing in the *Shaw* racial-gerrymandering cases to the treatment of standing in political-gerrymandering cases. In Gill v. Whitford, 138 S. Ct. 1916 (2018), the plaintiffs filed a suit claiming that the state legislative redistricting plan drafted by the legislature unconstitutionally diluted Democratic voters' voting strength statewide in violation of the equal protection clause and the First Amendment. (*Gill* is considered at greater length in the supplement to page 114 of the Main Volume.)

The Court, in an opinion by Chief Justice Roberts, held that the plaintiffs had not yet provided sufficient evidence of a concrete and particularized injury to establish Article III standing. It emphasized that the right to vote is "individual and personal in nature," and thus a plaintiff's claim that his voting strength has been diluted is "district specific." Citing *Hays*, the Court emphasized that a voter can assert a concrete claim only with respect to the district in which he lives. Thus, it rejected the assertion that the plaintiffs' claims were statewide in nature:

Here, the plaintiffs' partisan gerrymandering claims turn on allegations that their votes have been diluted. That harm arises from the particular composition of the voter's own district, which causes his vote—having been packed or cracked—to carry less weight than it would carry in another, hypothetical district. Remedying the individual voter's harm, therefore, does not necessarily require restructuring all of the State's legislative districts. It requires revising only such districts as are necessary to reshape the voter's district—so that the voter may be unpacked or uncracked, as the case may be.

And the Court rejected the claim that the plaintiffs had suffered impairment of their interest in the overall composition of the legislature: "[O]ur cases to date have not found that this presents an individual and personal injury of the kind required for Article III standing. On the facts of this case, the plaintiffs may not rely on 'the kind of undifferentiated, generalized grievance about the conduct of government that we have refused to countenance in the past.' A citizen's interest in the overall composition of the legislature is embodied in his right to vote for his representative. And the citizen's abstract interest in policies adopted by the legislature on the facts here is a nonjusticiable 'general interest common to all members of the public.' *Ex parte Levitt,* 302 U.S. 633, 634 (1937) (*per curiam*)."

VI
IMPLIED
FUNDAMENTAL
RIGHTS

E. Fundamental Interests and the Equal Protection Clause

Page 792. At the end of the Note, add the following:

The Court again avoided a decision on the merits concerning partisan gerrymandering in Gill v. Whitford, 138 S. Ct. 1916 (2018). (*Gill* is considered at greater length in the supplement to page 114 of the Main Volume.) In a 9-0 decision, the Court, per Chief Justice Roberts, held that the individual plaintiffs had failed to prove that they had standing. The Court remanded the case in order to give the plaintiffs the opportunity to demonstrate standing. In a companion case, Benisek v. Lamone, 138 S. Ct. 1942 (2018), the Court, in a per curiam opinion, held that a district judge did not abuse his equitable discretion in denying a preliminary injunction to plaintiffs complaining about partisan gerrymandering.

Should there be a per se constitutional prohibition on the use of partisan considerations in making districting decisions? For a positive answer that ties the response to bans on partisanship in other areas of constitutional law, see Michael S. Kang, Gerrymandering and the Constitutional Norm against Government Partisanship, 116 Mich. L. Rev. 351 (2017).

G.   Procedural Due Process

Page 936.   At the end of section 2 of the Note, add the following:

Can the *Din* Court's treatment of the liberty interest in marriage unification be reconciled with its treatment of the liberty to marry in Obergefell v. Hodges (page 900 of the Main Volume)? For a discussion, see Abrams, The Rights of Marriage: *Obergefell, Din,* and the Future of Constitutional Family Law, 103 Cornell L. Rev. 501 (2018).

H.   The Contracts and Takings Clauses

Page 965.   Before section 4 of the Note, add the following:

For yet another rejection of a contract clause claim, see Sveen v. Melin, 138 S. Ct. 1815 (2018). In 1998, Sveen purchased a life insurance policy and named his wife, Melin, as the primary beneficiary. After the policy had been purchased, Minnesota enacted a statute providing that a divorce revokes the designation of a former spouse as a beneficiary. However, the statute operated only as a default rule; a divorce decree could direct that the former spouse remain the beneficiary, or the policyholder could override the revocation.

Sveen and Melin divorced in 2007 and, because the decree made no mention of the insurance policy and Sveen had not revised his beneficiary designation, the statute meant that the proceeds of the policy went to Sveen's contingent beneficiaries. Melin claimed that the statute violated the contract clause, but in an 8-1 decision, the Court, per Justice Kagan disagreed.

According to the Court, there was no need to decide whether the statute was an appropriate means to advance a "significant and legitimate public purpose," because the statute did not substantially impair a contractual obligation. This was true for three reasons. First, the statute was designed to reflect a policyholder's intent and, therefore supported rather than impaired the contractual scheme. Second, the statute was unlikely to disturb any policyholder's expectations because it did no more than what a divorce court might have done if the statute did not exist. Finally, the statute provided only a default rule that the policyholder could undo by renaming his former spouse as the beneficiary.

Justice Gorsuch filed a dissenting opinion.

VII
FREEDOM OF EXPRESSION

A. Introduction

Page 1015.   After the quote from John Stuart Mill, add the following:

More than two centuries before Mill's publication of *On Liberty*, John Milton offered somewhat similar observations about the freedom of speech in his *Areopagitica* (1644). Consider Blasi, A Reader's Guide to John Milton's *Areopagitica*, 2017 Sup. Ct. Rev. 273, 293, 298, in which Blasi explains that Milton maintained that freedom of inquiry requires "the liberty to know, to utter, and to argue freely." Indeed, among the most important features of Milton's argument "is the positive value he sees in confronting evil and dangerous ideas." In his view, "the search for understanding would be much worse off were those ideas not to be available as foils and provocations and were authors and readers not seasoned by the experience of engaging them."

Page 1020.   At the end of the paragraph at the top of the page, add the following:

Consider Kendrick, Use Your Words: On the "Speech" in "Freedom of Speech," 116 Mich. L. Rev. 667, 668 (2018):

> "Freedom of speech" is clearly important in American society. But what is it? Is free speech implicated when a bakery denies service to a same-sex couple shopping for a wedding cake? Is it implicated when a town applies a zoning ordinance to a tattoo parlor? . . .
>
> Most people presented with the question would say that free speech has something to do with activities that we colloquially call speaking, and that these activities are important in some way. But when serving a cake is speech, and tattooing is speech, [we] might wonder whether we have strayed rather far from both the notion of "speech" as a phenomenon and from whatever it is that might made "freedom of speech" important as a legal, political, or moral right. This matters, [because] if freedom of speech is a basic human right, we ought to be able to articulate when it is implicated and when it is not.

B.   Content-Based Restrictions: Dangerous Ideas and Information

Page 1060.   At the end of section b of the Note, add the following:

6c. Tsesis, Terrorist Speech on Social Media, 70 Vand. L. Rev. 651, 654-55, 707 (2017):

> The Internet is awash with calls for terrorism. [Technically] adept terrorist organizations and their devotees exploit

social networking sites to spread ideologies, disseminate instructional videos, consolidate power, and threaten enemies. [Twitter is] an active forum for a variety of terror organizations [and] YouTube is likewise a hub for radical videos available for viewing throughout the world. [In addressing this challenge, some commentators] believe that courts should unfailingly adhere to the *Brandenburg* standard; according to this perspective, only imminently harmful terrorist speech is subject to censure. But this perspective lacks the nuance to distinguish speech made at a private meeting, attended by a few Ku Klux Klan members in that case, and the national — indeed the global — reach of internet terrorist advocacy. [A] federal law against terrorist incitement [is] the most robust way to address the threat of terrorist propaganda on social media while staying true to free speech doctrine.

Page 1074.   At the end of the first paragraph of section 9 of the Note, add the following, after the citation to Tsesis:

Wright, The Heckler's Veto Today, 68 Case W. Res. L. Rev. 159 (2017); Russomanno, Speech on Campus: How America's Crisis in Confidence Is Eroding Free Speech Values, 45 Hastings Const. L.Q. 273 (2018).

Page 1075.   At the end of section 9 of the Note, add the following:

For another facet of the "heckler's veto" issue, consider the issue of heckling itself. To what extent does the First Amendment protect the right of audience members to disrupt a speech by making noise? Suppose instead they "heckle" the speaker with uninvited questions and challenges? In such speech protected by the First Amendment even if it interrupts the speaker? In what circumstances can such heckling constitutionally be prohibited? See Waldron, Heckle: To Disconcert with Questions, Challenges, or Gibes, 2017 Sup. Ct. Rev. 1.

Page 1081.   **At the end of the paragraph beginning with the words "On June 22," add the following:**

For a fuller account of the Skokie controversy, see P. Strum, When the Nazis Came to Skokie (1999).

Page 1082.   **At the beginning of the paragraph beginning with the words "On the hate speech issue," add the following:**

For a more critical account of the actual effect of hate speech laws in other nations, see N. Strossen, Hate: Why We Should Resist It with Free Speech, Not Censorship (2018).

C. *Overbreadth, Vagueness, and Prior Restraint*

Page 1111.   **At the end of the paragraph discussing Walker v. City of Birmingham, add the following:**

For a critical analysis of the Court's 5-4 decision in *Walker*, see Kennedy, Walker v. City of Birmingham Revisited, 2017 Sup. Ct. Rev. 313, 336:

That people were compelled to resort to political protest to challenge the widespread and blatant racial discrimination in mid-twentieth century America was disgraceful. That they were arrested and jailed by local authorities intent upon suppressing their message is outrageous. That this persecution was then blessed by the United States Supreme Court was tragic. . . . Of all the places to proclaim the civilizing hand of the law, the Supreme Court chose a case that absolved judicial white supremacists and relegated to jail Martin Luther King, Jr.

D. Content-Based Restrictions: "Low" Value

Page 1162. At the end of section 6 of the Note, add the following:

See Redish and Voils, False Commercial Speech and the First Amendment, 25 Wm. & Mary Bill Rts. J. 765 (2017).

Page 1164. At the end of the first paragraph on the page, add the following:

For a lively account of the life and times of Anthony Comstock, see A. Werbel, Lust on Trial (2018).

Page 1195. At the end of Section 6, following the citation to Lakier, add the following:

Is the Court's sharp distinction between high-value and low-value speech too rigid and artificial? Would it be better for the Court to use strict scrutiny only for truly high-value speech, deferential review for low-value speech, and intermediate scrutiny for all types of speech in-between? See Han, Middle-Value Speech, 61 S. Cal. L. Rev. 65 (2017).

Page 1221.   At the end of section e of the Note, add the following:

For the argument that laws forbidding hate speech undermine the political legitimacy of laws prohibiting discrimination, see Weinstein, Hate Speech Bans, Democracy, and Political Legitimacy, 32 Const. Comm. 527 (2017).

Page 1223.   After section j of the Note, add the following:

k. N. Strossen, Hate: Why We Should Resist It with Free Speech, Not Censorship 81, 87, 99 (2018):

[Laws] censoring "hate speech" have predictably been enforced against those who lack political power, including government critics and members of the very minority groups these laws are intended to protect. This concern has been raised repeatedly by international human rights organizations. For example, the [2015 report by the European Commission Against Racism and Intolerance] observed that although "the duty under international law to criminalize certain forms of hate speech . . . was established to protect members of vulnerable minority groups," members of these groups have "been disproportionately the subject of prosecutions" under European "hate speech" laws.

[For example, although] the 1965 British "hate speech" law was passed to quell growing racism against minority groups, the first person convicted under it was a black man who cursed a white police officer. [Similarly,] Canadian "hate speech" laws also have been enforced to suppress expression of minority speakers and views. [In one instance, for example,] Canadian Customs seized 1,500 copies of a book that various Canadian universities had tried to import from the United States. What was this dangerous racist, sexist book? None other than *Black Looks: Race and Representation*, by the African-American feminist scholar, bell hooks. [And in] 2017, the Austrian Court of Appeal affirmed a lower court ruling that anonymous Facebook posts criticizing Austria's Green Party leader [constituted] illegal "hate speech" [because they called her a] "lousy traitor" and "corrupt bumpkin."

E. *Content-Neutral Restrictions: Limitations on the Means of Communication and the Problem of Content Neutrality*

Page 1245.   At the end of the material on Kovacs v. Cooper, add the following:

Consider the issue of "heckling." Suppose members of the audience at a speech on public or private property decide to "heckle" the speaker. In what circumstances can the government constitutionally order the hecklers to stop? Assuming the government is acting in a content-neutral manner, how should the rule be fashioned? Can the state constitutionally ban all heckling insofar as the speaker objects to it? Should it matter whether the hecklers are (a) attempting to disrupt the event and prevent the speech, or (b) asking hard questions and posing challenges to the speaker, even if she doesn't want to be interrupted? To what extent do members of the audience have a First Amendment right (a) to disrupt the event or (b) to heckle the speaker by asking uninvited questions and making uninvited comments? What is the right First Amendment standard for addressing such situations? For a lively discussion of heckling, see Waldron, Heckle: To Disconcert with Questions, Challenges, or Gibes, 2017 Sup. Ct. Rev. 1.

Page 1273.　At the end of section 2 of the Note at the top of the page, add the following:

Consider Krotoszynski, Our Shrinking First Amendment: On the Growing Problem of Reduced Access to Public Property for Speech Activity, 78 Ohio St. L.J. 779, 804, 817 (2017): "[T]he Rehnquist and Roberts Court have reset the balance in the government's favor and have done so to a significant degree. Access to government property for expressive purposes is considerably more circumscribed today than it was in the 1960s or 1970s. [A] course correction that places a higher burden of justification on the government for resisting free speech easements on public property would better serve our core commitment to freedom of expression as an essential condition for democratic self-government to flourish."

Page 1284.　At the end of section 2 of the Note, add the following:

3. *The reach of* Lehman: *polling places.* In Minnesota Voters Alliance v. Mansky, 138 S. Ct. 1876 (2018), the Court considered the constitutionality of a state law prohibiting individuals, including voters, from wearing a "political badge, political button, or other political insignia" inside a polling booth on Election Day. Unlike Burson v. Freeman, noted at page 1279 of the Main Volume, which prohibited the display or distribution of campaign materials within one hundred feet of a polling place, and thus restricted

speech in a public forum, the law in *Minnesota Voters Alliance* was limited only to speech within a polling place. The Court thus concluded that it regulated speech in a nonpublic forum. In such circumstances, the Court explained that the "government may reserve such a forum 'for its intended purposes, [as] long as the regulation on speech is reasonable and not an effort to suppress expression merely because public officials oppose the speaker's view.'"

Applying that test, the Court reasoned that there was "no basis for rejecting Minnesota's determination that some forms of advocacy should be excluded from the polling place." Nonetheless, the Court invalidated the Minnesota law, because even though it served a reasonable purpose and even though it was applied in an even-handed manner, the restriction was too ill-defined to give reasonable guidance to election officials to enable them to apply the law in a reasonably consistent and predictable manner. The Court noted, for example, that it was unclear whether badges, insignias, or buttons were forbidden if they supported the ACLU, said "All Lives Matter," endorsed the NRA, or quoted the First Amendment. The Court therefore concluded that "if a State wishes to set its polling place apart as areas free of partisan discord, it must employ a more discernible approach than the one Minnesota has offered here."

Page 1317.   At the end of section 3 of the Note, add the following:

4. *How much should it matter whether the public thinks it is seeing "government speech"?* Consider Hemel and Ouellette, Public Perceptions of Government Speech, 2017 Sup. Ct. Rev. 33, 35-36:

> To draw the line between government speech and private expression, the Supreme Court's early government speech cases looked to whether the speaker is a "traditional" government

agency or official and to whether the government exercises "control over the message." [In its more recent decisions, however, such as *Summum, Walker,* and *Matal*], the Court has placed increasing emphasis on whether members of the public reasonably perceive the relevant expression as government speech. [While] there are strong theoretical reasons to draw the line between government speech and private speech on the basis of public perception, the Court has so far failed to develop a reliable method for determining whether the public perceives expression to be government speech. [It] would seem that the best way to resolve the worry is to ask a representative sample of the population.

The authors conducted a national survey to test the accuracy of some of the Court's assumptions. They found that some "of the speculative claims made by the Justices," such as the assumption in *Summum* that members of the public interpret monuments on government land as conveying a message on the government's behalf, were borne out by their survey, whereas other claims made by the Justices, such as the assumption in *Matal* that members of the public do not treat federal registration of trademarks as government speech, were not confirmed by their survey. The authors also found that individuals are more likely to attribute messages to the government when they agree with the message. Are such surveys a sound way to decide whether the message communicated should be deemed government speech? If not, is there a better way to make such judgments?

Page 1326. At the end of section 5 of the Note, add the following:

For a recent analysis of the incidental effects doctrine, see Coenen, Free Speech and Generally Applicable Laws: A New Doctrinal Synthesis, 103 Iowa L. Rev. 435 (2018).

Page 1350.   At the end of section 3 of the Note, add the following:

3a. *Wedding cakes.* Masterpiece Cakeshop v. Colorado Civil Rights Comm'n, 138 S. Ct. 1719 (2018), posed the question whether a state law prohibiting discrimination on the basis of sexual orientation could constitutionally require a baker who opposes same-sex marriage to sell a wedding cake to a same-sex couple. (The case is also considered at the supplement to page 1519 of the Main Volume.) The baker argued that for the state to compel him to make such a cake would violate both his freedom of speech and freedom of religion. On the speech issue, the baker maintained that for the state to compel him to make such a cake would require him to express a message he personally rejects. In assessing his claim, should it matter whether the couple simply wanted to buy a pre-made wedding cake from the baker? Whether they wanted the baker to make a cake with figures of two men on top of the cake? Whether they wanted the cake to include the words "Congratulations Charlie and Dave!!"? Would those who see the cake be likely to attribute its message to the baker? Should that matter?

The Supreme Court avoided deciding the compelled speech question, although in his opinion for the Court Justice Kennedy observed: "The free speech aspect of this case is difficult, for few persons who [see] a beautiful wedding cake [would think] of its creation as an exercise of protected speech." But, he added: "If a baker refused to design a special cake with words or images celebrating the marriage, [that] might be different from a refusal to sell any cake at all. In deciding whether a baker's creation can be protected, these details might make a difference."

Although the Court did not decide the compelled speech question, Justice Thomas, in a concurring opinion joined by Justice Gorsuch, argued that the application of the statute to the baker in this case compelled him to convey a message he did not want to convey. Although conceding that the mere act of producing and selling wedding cakes is not in itself necessarily expressive behavior, Thomas argued that in this case the baker's act of "creating and designing custom wedding cakes [is] expressive." This was so, he maintained, because the baker "considers himself an artist," he "takes exceptional care with each cake that he creates," and a wedding cake's "primary purpose" is not so much to be eaten, as "to mark the beginning of a new marriage and to celebrate the couple." Thus, by forcing the baker "to create custom wedding cakes for same-sex weddings," the challenged law "requires him to, at the very least, acknowledge that same-sex weddings are 'weddings' and suggest that they should be celebrated—the precise message he believes his faith forbids." Invoking *Hurley*, Thomas concluded that the "First Amendment prohibits [the state] from requiring" the baker "to 'affir[m] . . . a belief with which [he] disagrees.' "

3b. *State-mandated notices in "crisis pregnancy centers."* In National Institute of Family and Life Advocates v. Becerra, ___ S. Ct. ___ (2018), the Court considered the constitutionality of the California Reproductive Freedom, Accountability, Comprehensive Care, and Transparency Act (FACT Act), which provides that licensed medical facilities that provide women with assistance involving pregnancy or family planning must post a notice informing their patients that "California has public programs that provide immediate free or low-cost access to comprehensive family planning services, prenatal care, and abortion for eligible women." The Act provides further that unlicensed clinics offering similar services must post a notice making clear that California has not licensed the clinics to provide medical services. The stated purpose of the FACT Act was to "ensure that California residents make their personal reproductive health care decisions knowing their rights and the health care services available to them."

The FACT Act was challenged by two "crisis pregnancy centers," one licensed and one unlicensed. "Crisis pregnancy centers" are "pro-life" organizations that offer a limited range of free options to women but, according to the state, "aim to discourage and prevent women from seeking abortions." There are approximately 200 such centers in California. The crisis pregnancy centers that challenged the Act maintained that the requirement that they post the mandated notices abridged their freedom of speech. The District Court denied their motion for a preliminary injunction, and the Ninth Circuit affirmed.

The Supreme Court, in a 5-4 decision, reversed. Justice Thomas delivered the opinion of the Court:

> The licensed notice is a content-based regulation of speech. By compelling individuals to speak a particular message, such notices "alte[r] the content of [their] speech." [Here], for example, licensed clinics must provide a government-drafted script about the availability of state-sponsored services, as well as contact information for how to obtain them. One of those services is abortion—the very practice that petitioners are devoted to opposing. By requiring petitioners to inform women how they can obtain state-subsidized abortions—at the same time petitioners try to dissuade women from choosing that option—the licensed notice plainly "alters the content" of petitioners' speech.

The Court thus held that "strict scrutiny" was the appropriate standard in this case. Because the lower courts, which characterized the law as a regulation of "professional" speech, applied a less demanding standard of review, the Court reversed, noting that the Act could not pass muster under the proper—and more demanding—standard of review.

Justice Breyer, joined by Justices Ginsburg, Sotomayor, and Kagan, dissented. Breyer maintained that the Court's decision was clearly inconsistent with past precedents. In Planned Parenthood v. Casey, 505 U.S. 833 (1992), for example, the Court upheld a state law that required doctors to inform women considering an abortion about the nature of the abortion procedure, the health risks of abortion and of childbirth, and the availability of printed materials describing the fetus, medical assistance for childbirth, potential child support, and the agencies that would provide adoption services (and other alternatives to abortion). Similarly, in Zauderer v. Office of Disciplinary Counsel, 471 U.S. 626 (1985), the Court upheld a disciplinary rule requiring attorneys to disclose in their advertisements that clients would have to pay "costs" even if their lawsuits were unsuccessful. Breyer maintained that these and other precedents made clear that "professional" speech, of the sort involved in this case, could be regulated consistent with the First Amendment under the more deferential standard of review applied by the lower courts, and that the Court was wrong to apply strict scrutiny in this case.

In light of this decision, what should be the outcome in cases that involve laws requiring organizations that perform legal abortions to advise patients about alternative ways to deal with unwanted pregnancies? See, e.g., Texas Medical Providers Performing Abortion Services v. Lakey, 667 F.3d 570 (5th Cir. 2012) (upholding a Texas law that prohibits a woman from getting an abortion unless her physician first performs an ultrasound, places the ultrasound images in her view, describes the images to her, makes fetal heart sounds audible, if possible, and describes those sounds to her, whether or not she wants to see or hear them).

Page 1350.   Replace section 5 of the Note with the following:

5. *Union dues.* May a state compel government employees to pay union dues? In Abood v. Detroit Board of Education, 431 U.S. 209 (1977), the Court upheld a state statute authorizing unions representing government employees to charge members dues insofar as the dues are used to support collective bargaining and related activities, but invalidating the statute insofar as the union uses the dues "to contribute to political candidates and to express political views unrelated to its duties as exclusive bargaining representative."

In subsequent decisions, the Court refined this holding. See Ellis v. Brotherhood of Railway, Airline & Steamship Clerks, 466 U.S. 85 (1984) (compelled contributions may constitutionally be used to pay for union conventions, social activities, and publications); Keller v. State Bar of California, 496 U.S. 1 (1990) (an integrated state bar association may not use compulsory dues to finance political and ideological activities with which particular members disagree when such expenditures are not "necessarily or reasonably incurred for the purpose of regulating the legal profession or improving the quality of legal services"); Lehnert v. Ferris Faculty Association, 500 U.S. 507 (1991) (a union may constitutionally charge dissenting employees only for those activities that are (1) "germane" to collective bargaining; (2) justified by the government's interests in labor peace and avoiding free riders; and (3) not significantly burdening of speech); Davenport v. Washington Education Association, 551 U.S. 177 (2007) (a state may constitutionally require public-sector unions to receive affirmative authorization from nonmembers before spending their agency fees for election-related purposes); Knox v. Service Employees International Union, 567 U.S. 310 (2012) (when a public-sector union imposes a special assessment or mid-year dues increase, the union cannot constitutionally require nonmembers to pay the increased amount unless they choose to opt in by affirmatively consenting).

In Harris v. Quinn, 134 S. Ct. 2618 (2014), the Court, in a 5-4 decision, seriously called *Abood* into question, but found it unnecessary to resolve the issue. In Janus v. American Federation of State, County, and Municipal Employees, 138 S. Ct. 2448 (2018), however, the Court, in another 5-4 decision, overruled *Abood*, holding that the state cannot constitutionally compel its employees to pay dues to public-sector labor unions that represent them, even if the dues are limited to paying only for collective bargaining and other activities designed to benefit all employees. Writing for the Court, Justice Alito maintained that it violates the First Amendment for the state to compel individuals to pay fees "to endorse ideas they find objectionable" unless the government can satisfy the standard of "exacting scrutiny." Alito reasoned that neither the state's interest in preserving "labor peace" nor its interest in avoiding "free riders" was sufficient to meet this standard. Henceforth, Alito concluded, "neither an agency fee nor any other payment to the union may be deducted from a nonmember's wages, nor may any other attempt be made to collect such a payment, unless the employee affirmatively consents to pay."

Justice Kagan, joined by Justices Ginsburg, Breyer and Sotomayor, dissented:

> For over 40 years, [*Abood*] struck a stable balance between public employees' First Amendment rights and government entities' interests in running their workforces as they thought proper. Under that decision, a government entity could require public employees to pay a fair share of the cost that a union incurs when negotiating on their behalf over terms of employment. But no part of that fair-share payment could go to any of the union's political or ideological activities.

> [The] Court's decisions have long made plain that government entities have substantial latitude to regulate their employees' speech—especially about terms of employment—in the interest of operating their workplaces effectively. *Abood* allowed governments to do just that. While protecting public employees' expression about non-workplace matters, the decision enabled a government to advance important managerial interests—by ensuring the presence of an exclusive employee representative to bargain with.

> Not any longer. [Today's] decision will have large-scale consequences. Public employee unions will lose a secure source of financial support. State and local governments that thought fair-share provisions furthered their interests will need to find new ways of managing their work-forces. Across the country, the relationships of public employees

and employers will alter in both predictable and wholly unexpected ways.

Rarely if ever has the Court overruled a decision — let alone one of this import — with so little regard for the usual principles of *stare decisis*. There are no special justifications for reversing *Abood*. It has proved workable. No recent developments have eroded its underpinnings. And it is deeply entrenched, in both the law and the real world. More than 20 States have statutory schemes built on the decision. Those laws underpin thousands of ongoing contracts involving millions of employees. Reliance interests do not come any stronger than those surrounding *Abood*. And likewise, judicial disruption does not get any greater than what the Court does today.

Page 1385.   At the end of section a of the Note, add the following:

aa. A. Winkler, We the Corporations 372-73 (2018):

[As a result of *Citizens United*, corporate] spending in the next presidential election cycle of 2012 rose dramatically. Corporations were now allowed to spend general treasury funds to finance independent expenditures in favor of, or against, candidates for office. They also gained the right to contribute to "Super PACs" — a special type of political action committee that [was] able to accept unlimited contributions from corporations. [The] Center for Public Integrity [estimated] that in 2012 there was nearly $1 billion in new political spending [from corporations and individuals] traceable to *Citizens United*. . . .

The *Citizens United* decision [triggered] a public backlash. Polls showed that eight in ten Americans were opposed to the Supreme Court's decision. The opposition crossed party lines, with 85 percent of Democrats, 76 percent of Republicans, and 81 percent of Independents saying *Citizens United* was wrongly decided.

F. Freedom of the Press

Page 1415.   At the end of section 1 of the Note, add the following:

In *Branzburg*, the Court recognized the awkwardness in holding that the First Amendment gives the press special rights. Part of the difficulty is the challenge of deciding who gets to assert the special rights of the press. But suppose the government wants to give special privileges to "the press." Can it constitutionally do so?

In *Citizens United*, the five justices in the majority maintained that the statutory provision in the Campaign Finance Act that exempted media-corporations (like *The New York Times*) from restrictions on campaign expenditures that applied to non-media-corporations (like General Motors) violated the First Amendment, because such a distinction between different types of corporations was "dangerous, and unacceptable." 558 U.S., at 351. Is this persuasive?

Consider West, Favoring the Press, 106 Cal. L. Rev. 91, 94-95 (2018):

> [This] nondiscrimination view of the Press Clause is deeply flawed for the simple reason that the press is different and has always been recognized as such. [Indeed,] the legislative practice of determining that the press should be favored in some contexts, so as to further a public good, dates back to the birth of the nation. Since then, federal and state

legislatures, courts, and other government actors have adopted a wide range of regulations that are not granted to other speakers. These measures include testimonial privileges; enhanced protections from searches and seizures; [special] access to government-controlled placed, information, or meetings; [preferred] postal rates; [and so on]. It is [entirely] in keeping with the text, history, and spirit of the First Amendment's Press Clause for the government to, at times, treat press speakers differently.

Page 1427.   At the end of section d of the Note, add the following:

e. *Net neutrality*. Consider Bhagwat, When Speech Is Not "Speech," 78 Ohio. St. L.J. 839, 857 (2017):

> The basic concern driving net neutrality is that broadband providers, because they possess substantial market power and control bottlenecks that end users must pass through to access the Internet, can use their power to interfere with an open Internet where end users and edge providers can communicate with each other without interference or preferentialism. To prevent that, [the FCC in 2005 adopted net neutrality rules that prohibited] broadband providers from blocking access to particular websites, slowing down access to particular websites, or engaging in "paid prioritization" whereby broadband providers favor some Internet traffic over other traffic in exchange for compensation.

Is the requirement of net neutrality consistent with the First Amendment? Consider cases like *Red Lion*, *Tornillo*, and *Turner*. See U.S. Telecom Ass'n v. FCC, 825 F.3d 674 (D.C. Cir. 2016) (upholding the constitutionality of the FCC's net neutrality rule). In 2018, the FCC proposed repealing the requirement of net neutrality.

Page 1428.   At the end of section 5 of the Note, add the following:

For an argument in support of such a change in Section 230, see Citron and Wittes, The Internet Will Not Break: Denying Bad Samaritans § 230 Immunity, 86 Fordham L. Rev. 401 (2017).

Page 1429.   At the end of section 6 of the Note, add the following:

Consider also Citron, Extremist Speech, Compelled Conformity, and Censorship Creep, 93 Notre Dame L. Rev. 1035 (2018):

> Silicon Valley has long been viewed as a full-throated champion of First Amendment values. [But in] an agreement with the European Commission, the dominant tech companies have [recently altered their] policies [in order] to stave off threatened European regulation. Far more than illegal speech or violent terrorist imagery is in EU lawmakers' sights, as too is online radicalization and "fake news." [The] impact of [such] coercion will be far reaching. Unlike national laws that are limited to geographic borders, terms-of-service agreements apply to platforms' services on a global scale. [These] changes are less the result of market choices [by private entities] than of a bowing to [foreign] government pressure.

How should the United States address such potentially powerful foreign influence on American free expression?

7. *The fragility of the free press.* Consider Jones & West, The Fragility of the Free American Press, 112 Nw. U. L. Rev. 567 (2017):

The President of the United States has boldly declared an all-out "war" on the press, and his primary weapon has been an attack on tradition. Repeatedly and aggressively, President Donald Trump has flouted press-protecting norms and customs that have been long respected by other presidents. [He] has ignored customary media accommodations, criticized or excluded reporters and news organization perceived as unfriendly, spoken of the press in disparaging and vilifying terms, and even threatened media organizations with lawsuits and retributive governmental actions.

Journalists and scholars have rightly warned us that President Trump's disrespect for the Fourth Estate is troubling and that it threatens to harm the vitality of this important check on our democracy. As grave as these warnings have been, however, they have fallen short of capturing the true seriousness of the situation. This is because the kind of press we value and need in the United States — one that is free, independent, and democracy-enhancing — does not just occur naturally. Nor is it protected by a single, robust constitutional right. Rather, our free press sits atop an increasingly fragile edifice. This edifice is supported by a number of legal and nonlegal pillars, such as the institutional media's relative financial strength, the goodwill of the public, a mutually dependent relationship with government officials, and the back of sympathetic judges. Each of these supports, however, has weakened substantially in recent years, leaving one remaining pillar to bear more of the weight. That final pillar is political tradition — a set of customs that demands the President of the United States recognize and respect the vital role of the press. It is this final pillar that Trump has put in his sights.

VIII
THE CONSTITUTION
AND RELIGION

B. *The Establishment Clause*

Page 1487.   Before the Note, add the following:

TRUMP v. HAWAII

138 S. Ct. 2392 (2018)

CHIEF JUSTICE ROBERTS delivered the opinion of the Court. . . .

[One week after taking office, President Trump signed an executive order directing the Secretary of Homeland Security to conduct a review of the adequacy of information provided by foreign governments about their nationals seeking entry into the United States. Pending the review, the order suspended the entry of foreign nationals for ninety days from seven predominantly Muslim countries.

[The order produced widespread confusion and protest, and a district court temporarily enjoined it, a decision affirmed by the Court of Appeals. Rather than proceeding further with litigation, the President revoked the order and replaced it with a new order again requiring a worldwide review and temporarily restricting entry (with case-by-case waivers) of foreign nationals from six predominantly Muslim countries. Courts again temporarily enjoined enforcement of the order, but the Supreme Court stayed these injunctions with respect to foreign nationals who lacked "a credible claim of a bona fide relationship with a person or entity in the United States. Trump v. International Refugee Assistance Project, 137 S. Ct. 2080 (2017).

[Upon completion of the world-wide review, the President entered a third order, placing entry restrictions on the nationals of eight foreign states—Chad, Iran, Iraq, Libya, North Korea, Syria, Venezuela, and Yemen. Six of the states are predominantly Muslim. According to the order, the states were selected based upon a review of the methods they utilized to determine whether individuals seeking entry into the United States posed a security threat. The order exempted foreign nationals who had been granted asylum and provided for case-by-case waivers. The state of Hawaii and three individuals brought suit challenging the legality of the order.]

III

[In this section of the opinion, the Court held that the order was justified under power delegated to the President in the Immigration and Naturalization Act]

IV

A

[The Court held that the plaintiffs have standing to raise the claim. This issue is discussed in the supplement to page 118 of the Main Volume]

B

[Plaintiffs argued that the order violated the establishment clause because it operated as a "religious gerrymander" that singled out Muslims because of religious animus. They claimed that the stated reasons for the order were pretextual.

[In support of their argument they relied upon the following facts, many of which are detailed in Justice Sotomayor's dissenting opinion:

- Before he was elected, Candidate Trump stated that he was "calling for a total and complete shutdown of Muslims entering the United States until our country's representatives can figure out what is going on. According to Pew Research, among others, there is great hatred towards Americans by large segments of the Muslim population. [Until] we are able to determine and understand this problem and the dangerous threat it poses, our country cannot be the victims of the horrendous attacks by people that believe only in Jihad, and have no sense of reason or respect for human life."
- Also during the campaign, Trump justified his proposal by saying that Franklin Roosevelt "did the same thing" with respect to internment of Japanese Americans during World War II; told an apocryphal story about General John J. Pershing killing a large group of Muslim insurgents in the Philippines with bullets dipped in pigs' blood; stated that "Islam hates us"; called for surveillance of mosques in the United States; and stated that Muslims "do not respect us at all."
- After signing the first version of the executive order, President Trump explained that Christians would be given priority for entry as refugees. He stated that the order was designed "to help" Christians in Syria.
- An advisor to President Trump told the media that "when [Donald Trump] first announced it, he said 'Muslim ban.' He called me up. He said, 'put a commission together. Show me the right way to do it legally.'"
- While litigation about the second order was pending, President Trump characterized it as a "watered down version of the first one" that had been tailored at the behest of "the lawyers." He stated that he would prefer to "go back to the first [order] and go all the way" and that it was "very hard" for Muslims to assimilate into Western culture. In a

tweet, he stated that "People, the lawyers and the courts can call it whatever they want, but I am calling it what we need and what it is, a TRAVEL BAN! That's right, we need a TRAVEL BAN for certain DANGEROUS countries, not some politically correct term that won't help protect our people."

- After the third order was promulgated, President Trump retweeted three anti-Muslim videos entitled "Muslims destroy a Statue of Virgin Mary!", "Islamist mob pushes teenage boy off roof and beats him to death!" and "Muslim migrants beats up Dutch boy on crutches!" When asked about the videos, the White House Deputy Press Secretary connected them to the order and stated that the "President has been talking about these security issues for years now, from the campaign trail to the White House" and "has addressed these issues with the travel order that he issued earlier this year."]

Our Presidents have frequently used their power to espouse the principles of religious freedom and tolerance on which this Nation was founded. In 1790 George Washington reassured the Hebrew Congregation of Newport, Rhode Island that "happily the Government of the United States . . . gives to bigotry no sanction, to persecution no assistance [and] requires only that they who live under its protection should demean themselves as good citizens." President Eisenhower, at the opening of the Islamic Center of Washington, similarly pledged to a Muslim audience that "America would fight with her whole strength for your right to have here your own church," declaring that "[t]his concept is indeed a part of America." And just days after the attacks of September 11, 2001, President George W. Bush returned to the same Islamic Center to implore his fellow Americans—Muslims and non-Muslims alike—to remember during their time of grief that "[t]he face of terror is not the true faith of Islam," and that America is "a great country because we share the same values of respect and dignity and human worth." Yet it cannot be denied that the Federal Government and the Presidents who have carried its laws into effect have — from the Nation's earliest days — performed unevenly in living up to those inspiring words.

Plaintiffs argue that this President's words strike at fundamental standards of respect and tolerance, in violation of our constitutional tradition. But the issue before us is not whether to denounce the statements. It is instead the significance of those statements in reviewing a Presidential directive, neutral on its face, addressing a matter within the core of executive responsibility. In doing so, we must consider not only the statements of a particular President, but also the authority of the Presidency itself.

The case before us differs in numerous respects from the conventional Establishment Clause claim. Unlike the typical suit involving religious displays or school prayer, plaintiffs seek to invalidate a national security directive regulating the entry of aliens abroad. Their claim accordingly raises a number of delicate issues regarding the scope of the constitutional right and the manner of proof. The Proclamation, moreover, is facially neutral toward religion. Plaintiffs therefore ask the Court to probe the sincerity of the stated justifications for the policy by reference to extrinsic statements — many of which were made before the President took the oath of office. These various aspects of plaintiffs' challenge inform our standard of review.

C

[In this section, the Court discusses previous decisions relating to entry into the country and national security considerations. It characterized those decisions as providing for a "circumscribed judicial inquiry" when denial of entry allegedly burdens the constitutional rights of U.S. citizens. The Court's role was limited to determining whether the Executive gave a "facially legitimate and bona fide reason for its action."]

A conventional application of [this principle] would put an end to our review. But the Government has suggested that it may be appropriate here for the inquiry to extend beyond the facial neutrality of the order. For our purposes today, we assume that we may look behind the face of the Proclamation to the extent of applying rational basis review. That standard of review considers whether the entry policy is plausibly related to the Government's stated objective to protect the country and improve vetting processes. As a result, we may consider plaintiffs' extrinsic evidence, but will uphold the policy so long as it can reasonably be understood to result from a justification independent of unconstitutional grounds.

D...

The Proclamation is expressly premised on legitimate purposes: preventing entry of nationals who cannot be adequately vetted and inducing other nations to improve their practices. The text says nothing about religion. Plaintiffs and the dissent nonetheless emphasize that five of the seven nations currently included in the Proclamation have Muslim-majority populations. Yet that fact alone does not support an inference of religious hostility, given that the policy covers just 8% of the world's Muslim population and is limited to countries that were previously designated by Congress or prior administrations as posing national security risks.

The Proclamation, moreover, reflects the results of a worldwide review process undertaken by multiple Cabinet officials and their agencies. Plaintiffs seek to discredit the findings of the review, pointing to deviations from the review's baseline criteria resulting in the inclusion of Somalia and omission of Iraq. But as the Proclamation explains, in each case the determinations were justified by the distinct conditions in each country. . . .

Three additional features of the entry policy support the Government's claim of a legitimate national security interest. First, since the President introduced entry restrictions in January 2017, three Muslim-majority countries—Iraq, Sudan, and Chad—have been removed from the list of covered countries. . . .

Second, for those countries that remain subject to entry restrictions, the Proclamation includes significant exceptions for various categories of foreign nationals. . . .

Third, the Proclamation creates a waiver program open to all covered foreign nationals seeking entry as immigrants or nonimmigrants. . . .

Finally, the dissent invokes Korematsu v. United States, 323 U.S. 214 (1944). [*Korematsu* is discussed at page 532 of the Main Volume.] Whatever rhetorical advantage the dissent may see in doing so, *Korematsu* has nothing to do with this case. The forcible relocation of U.S. citizens to concentration camps, solely and explicitly on the basis of race, is objectively unlawful and outside the scope of Presidential authority. But it is wholly inapt to liken that morally repugnant order to a facially neutral policy denying certain foreign nationals the privilege of admission. The entry suspension is an act that is well within executive authority and could have been taken by any other President—the only question is evaluating the actions of this particular President in promulgating an otherwise valid Proclamation. The dissent's reference to *Korematsu*, however, affords this Court the opportunity to make express what is already obvious: *Korematsu* was gravely wrong the day it was decided, has been overruled in the court of history, and—to be clear—"has no place in law under the Constitution." 323 U.S., at 248 (Jackson, J., dissenting).

* * *

Under these circumstances, the Government has set forth a sufficient national security justification to survive rational basis review. We express no view on the soundness of the policy. We simply hold today that plaintiffs have not demonstrated a likelihood of success on the merits of their constitutional claim. The case now returns to the lower courts for such further proceedings as may be appropriate.

JUSTICE KENNEDY, concurring.

I join the Court's opinion in full. There may be some common ground between the opinions in this case, in that the Court does acknowledge that in some instances, governmental action may be subject to judicial review to determine whether or not it is "inexplicable by anything but animus," which in this case would be animosity to a religion. Whether judicial proceedings may properly continue in this case, in light of the substantial deference that is and must be accorded to the Executive in the conduct of foreign affairs, and in light of today's decision, is a matter to be addressed in the first instance on remand.

[In] all events, it is appropriate to make this further observation. There are numerous instances in which the statements and actions of Government officials are not subject to judicial scrutiny or intervention. That does not mean those officials are free to disregard the Constitution and the rights it proclaims and protects. The oath that all officials take to adhere to the Constitution is not confined to those spheres in which the Judiciary can correct or even comment upon what those officials say or do. Indeed, the very fact that an official may have broad discretion, discretion free from judicial scrutiny, makes it all the more imperative for him or her to adhere to the Constitution and to its meaning and its promise.

The First Amendment prohibits the establishment of religion and promises the free exercise of religion. From these safeguards, and from the guarantee of freedom of speech, it follows there is freedom of belief and expression. It is an urgent necessity that officials adhere to these constitutional guarantees and mandates in all their actions, even in the sphere of foreign affairs. An anxious world must know that our Government remains committed always to the liberties the Constitution seeks to preserve and protect, so that freedom extends outward, and lasts.

[A concurring opinion by Justice Thomas and a dissenting opinion by Justice Breyer, in which Justice Kagan joined, have been omitted].

JUSTICE SOTOMAYOR, with whom JUSTICE GINSBURG joins, dissenting.

The United States of America is a Nation built upon the promise of religious liberty. Our Founders honored that core promise by embedding the principle of religious neutrality in the First

Amendment. The Court's decision today fails to safeguard that fundamental principle. It leaves undisturbed a policy first advertised openly and unequivocally as a "total and complete shutdown of Muslims entering the United States" because the policy now masquerades behind a façade of national-security concerns. But this repackaging does little to cleanse Presidential Proclamation No. 9645 of the appearance of discrimination that the President's words have created. Based on the evidence in the record, a reasonable observer would conclude that the Proclamation was motivated by anti-Muslim animus. That alone suffices to show that plaintiffs are likely to succeed on the merits of their Establishment Clause claim. The majority holds otherwise by ignoring the facts, misconstruing our legal precedent, and turning a blind eye to the pain and suffering the Proclamation inflicts upon countless families and individuals, many of whom are United States citizens. Because that troubling result runs contrary to the Constitution and our precedent, I dissent. . . .

I . . .

A . . .

The "clearest command" of the Establishment Clause is that the Government cannot favor or disfavor one religion over another. That is so, this Court has held, because such acts send messages to members of minority faiths "'that they are outsiders, not full members of the political community.'" To determine whether plaintiffs have proved an Establishment Clause violation, the Court asks whether a reasonable observer would view the government action as enacted for the purpose of disfavoring a religion. In answering that question, this Court has generally considered the text of the government policy, its operation, and any available evidence regarding "the historical background of the decision under challenge, the specific series of events leading to the enactment or official policy in question, and the legislative or administrative history, including contemporaneous statements made by" the decisionmaker.

B

1

[Justice Sotomayor summarizes the statements made by President Trump that are quoted above.]

2

As the majority correctly notes, "the issue before us is not whether to denounce" these offensive statements. Rather, the dispositive and narrow question here is whether a reasonable observer, presented with all "openly available data," the text and "historical context" of the Proclamation, and the "specific sequence of events" leading to it, would conclude that the primary purpose of the Proclamation is to disfavor Islam and its adherents by excluding them from the country. The answer is unquestionably yes. Taking all the relevant evidence together, a reasonable observer would conclude that the Proclamation was driven primarily by anti-Muslim animus, rather than by the Government's asserted national-security justifications. . . .

Notably, the Court recently found less pervasive official expressions of hostility and the failure to disavow them to be constitutionally significant. [citing Masterpiece Cakeshop v. Colorado Civil Rights Comm'n, excerpted in the supplement to page 1519 of the Main Volume]

Ultimately, what began as a policy explicitly "calling for a total and complete shutdown of Muslims entering the United States" has since morphed into a "Proclamation" putatively based on national-security concerns. But this new window dressing cannot conceal an unassailable fact: the words of the President and his advisers create the strong perception that the Proclamation is contaminated by impermissible discriminatory animus against Islam and its followers. . . .

[In Parts II and III of her opinion, Justice Sotomayor argues that the Court erred in applying rational basis review to the order, that even utilizing rational basis review, the order is unconstitutional, and that the requirements for a preliminary injunction had been satisfied.]

IV ...

In holding that the First Amendment gives way to an executive policy that a reasonable observer would view as motivated by animus against Muslims, the majority opinion upends this Court's precedent, repeats tragic mistakes of the past, and denies countless individuals the fundamental right of religious liberty. Just weeks ago, the Court rendered its decision in Masterpiece Cakeshop, which applied the bedrock principles of religious neutrality and tolerance in considering a First Amendment challenge to government action. Those principles should apply equally here. In both instances, the question is whether a government actor exhibited tolerance and neutrality in reaching a decision that affects individuals' fundamental religious freedom. But unlike in Masterpiece, where a state civil rights commission was found to have acted without "the neutrality that the Free Exercise Clause requires," the government actors in this case will not be held accountable for breaching the First Amendment's guarantee of religious neutrality and tolerance. Unlike in Masterpiece, where the majority considered the state commissioners' statements about religion to be persuasive evidence of unconstitutional government action the majority here completely sets aside the President's charged statements about Muslims as irrelevant. That holding erodes the foundational principles of religious tolerance that the Court elsewhere has so emphatically protected, and it tells members of minority religions in our country "'that they are outsiders, not full members of the political community.'"

Today's holding is all the more troubling given the stark parallels between the reasoning of this case and that of Korematsu v. United States, 323 U.S. 214 (1944). In *Korematsu*, the Court gave "a pass [to] an odious, gravely injurious racial classification" authorized by an executive order. Adarand Constructors, Inc. v. Peña, 515 U.S. 200, 275 (1995) (Ginsburg, J., dissenting). As here, the Government invoked an ill-defined national security threat to justify an exclusionary policy of sweeping proportion. As here, the exclusion order was rooted in dangerous stereotypes about, inter alia, a particular group's supposed inability to assimilate and desire to harm the United States. As here, the Government was unwilling to reveal its own intelligence agencies' views of the alleged security concerns to the very citizens it purported to protect. And as here, there was strong evidence that impermissible hostility and animus motivated the Government's policy. Although a majority of the Court in *Korematsu* was willing to uphold the Government's actions based on a barren invocation of national security, dissenting Justices warned of that decision's harm to our constitutional fabric. . . .

Today, the Court takes the important step of finally overruling *Korematsu*, denouncing it as "gravely wrong the day it was decided." This formal repudiation of a shameful precedent is laudable and long overdue. But it does not make the majority's decision here acceptable or right. By blindly accepting the Government's misguided invitation to sanction a discriminatory policy motivated by animosity toward a disfavored group, all in the name of a superficial claim of national security, the Court redeploys the same dangerous logic underlying *Korematsu* and merely replaces one "gravely wrong" decision with another. Our Constitution demands, and our country deserves, a Judiciary willing to hold the coordinate branches to account when they defy our most sacred legal commitments. Because the Court's decision today has failed in that respect, with profound regret, I dissent.

Note: The Meaning of Trump v. Hawaii

1. *The holding.* What does the Court hold with respect to the establishment clause?

2. *The standard of review.* The President's comments are among the matters the Court says "inform" the standard of review. Is that standard "mere" rationality, rationality with bite, or something else? The Court identifies the Proclamation's facial neutrality, its inclusion of only 8 percent of the world's Muslim population, and the interagency process that produced the Proclamation as

reasons supporting the Proclamation's rationality. Would those items be sufficient under "rationality with bite"?

3. *"Independent" justification.* The opinion says that the Court "will uphold the policy so long as it can reasonably be understood to result from a justification independent of unconstitutional grounds." Consider these possibilities: (1) The Court will uphold the policy if it would have been adopted even without the unconstitutional grounds (in this context, even if the President had never made his comments nor harbored impermissible motivations). (2) The Court will uphold the policy if there exists a justification independent of the unconstitutional grounds. The possibilities differ in that the first asks about the actual decision-maker while the second asks about a hypothetical decision-maker. Which possibility seems more consistent with the facts of the case? Which is more consistent with the rationales for deference to the executive in the context of national-security related decisions?

4. *The non-endorsement principle.* Why does the Court not apply the non-endorsement principle? What principled basis, if any, is there for distinguishing between the "typical" establishment clause suit and this case? Are the "issues regarding the scope of the constitutional right and the manner of proof" more "delicate" in this context than in the context of legislative prayers said to have been adopted for constitutionally impermissible reasons?

D. Permissible Accommodation

Page 1519.   After section 3 of the Note, add the following:

MASTERPIECE CAKESHOP LTD. v. COLORADO CIVIL RIGHTS COMM'N, 138 S. Ct. 1719 (2018). After Masterpiece Cakeshop refused to provide a cake to celebrate the out-of-state wedding of a gay couple because of the owner Jack Phillips's religious opposition to same-sex marriage, the Colorado

Civil Rights Commission found that the owner had violated the state's anti-discrimination act, which prohibits discrimination based on sexual orientation in a "place of business engaged in any sales to the public. . . ." The Supreme Court reversed the state appeals court's decision upholding the finding of a violation, relying on *Lukumi*.

Writing for the Court, Justice Kennedy said, "The Court's precedents make clear that the baker, in his capacity as the owner of a business serving the public, might have his right to the free exercise of religion limited by generally applicable laws. Still, the delicate question of when the free exercise of his religion must yield to an otherwise valid exercise of state power needed to be determined in an adjudication in which religious hostility on the part of the State itself would not be a factor in the balance the State sought to reach. When the Colorado Civil Rights Commission considered this case, it did not do so with the religious neutrality that the Constitution requires."

That neutrality "was compromised" in several ways. "One commissioner suggested that Phillips can believe 'what he wants to believe,' but cannot act on his religious beliefs 'if he decided to do business in the state.' . . . Standing alone, [this statement] might mean simply that a business cannot refuse to provide services based on sexual orientation, regardless of the proprietor's personal views. On the other hand, [it] might be seen as inappropriate as dismissive [showing] lack of due consideration for Phillips' free exercise rights and the dilemma he faced. In view of the comments that followed, the latter seems the more likely." Two months later, another commissioner stated, "Freedom of religion and religion has been used to justify all kinds of discrimination throughout history, whether it be slavery, whether it be the holocaust. [And] to me it is one of the most despicable pieces of rhetoric that people can use to [use] their religion to hurt others." Justice Kennedy observed, "To describe a man's faith as 'one of the most despicable pieces of rhetoric that people can use' is to disparage his religion in at least two distinct ways: by describing it as despicable, and also by characterizing it as merely rhetorical.

[The] commissioner even went so far as to compare Phillips' invocation and sincerely held religious believes to defenses of slavery and the Holocaust. This sentiment is inappropriate for a Commission charged with the solemn responsibility of fair and neutral enforcement of Colorado's anti-discrimination law." . . .

"Another indication of hostility is the difference in treatment between Phillips' case and the cases of other bakers who objected to a requested case on the basis of conscience and prevailed before the Commission." Those cases involved bakers who refused "to create cakes with images that conveyed disapproval of same-sex marriage, along with religious text. Each time, the [Commission] found that the baker acted lawfully [because] the requested cake including 'wording and images [the baker] deemed derogatory. . . .'"

According to the Court, "the Commission was obliged [to] proceed in a manner neutral toward and tolerant of Phillips' religious beliefs. [Phillips] was entitled to a neutral decisionmaker who would give full and fair consideration to his religious objection as he sought to assert it in all of the circumstances in which this case was presented, considered, and decided."

Justice Kagan, joined by Justice Breyer, concurred. Referring to the treatment of the bakers who refused to provide cakes disapproving same-sex marriage, she wrote, "the bakers did not single out [the customer] because of his religion, but instead treated him in the same way they would have treated anyone else." Justice Gorsuch, joined by Justice Alito, concurred as well, but disagreed with Justice Kagan's characterization of the other bakers' actions: "In both cases, the effect on the customer was the same: bakers refused service to persons who bore a statutorily protected trait (religious faith and sexual orientation.) But in both cases the bakers refused service intending only to honor a personal conviction." Justice Thomas, joined by Justice Gorsuch, wrote a concurring opinion addressing the free speech claims Phillips advanced.

Justice Ginsburg, joined by Justice Sotomayor, dissented, finding that the matters the Court referred to "do not evidence hostility to religion of the kind we have previously held to signal a free-exercise violation." With respect to the others bakers' actions,

"Change [Phillips's customers'] sexual orientation (or sex), and Phillips would have provided the cake. Change [the religion of the customer requesting cakes with derogatory messages] and the bakers would have been no more willing to comply with his request."

Note: The Implications of Masterpiece Cakeshop

1. *Evidence of hostility.* What standard does the Court use to determine that the Commission's actions were hostile to religion? Are the comments of the two Commissioners, which the Court observed were not repudiated by other Commissioners or the state court, susceptible of a non-hostile interpretation? What about the Commission's actions with respect to the bakers who refused to provide cakes with messages they deemed derogatory? In Trump v. Hawaii, 138 S. Ct. 2392 (2018), the Court held that comments by President Trump indicating hostility to Muslims affected the standard of review it applied to determine whether an executive order restricting entry into the United States by citizens of certain specified nations was constitutionally permissible. (The case is discussed at the supplement to page 1487 of the Main Volume.)

2. *The requirement of neutral and respectful consideration of Phillips's claim.* Suppose the Commission rejected Phillips's claim with an opinion saying, "We have deep respect for your convictions, but the state's anti-discrimination law is completely general and does not authorize us to make any exceptions to accommodate sincerely held religious beliefs." What result under *Smith*? Suppose the two Commissioners (out of five) made the comments cited by the Court, to support their assertion that it was a good policy for the anti-discrimination law to deny the Commission the authority to make exceptions. What result under *Smith*?

3. *The relevance of the finding that bakers who refused to provide cakes with derogatory messages were not held to violate the anti-discrimination law.* Does the Commission's refusal find that the bakers who refused to provide cakes with what they regarded as derogatory messages show that the Colorado statute

did authorize the Commission to make exceptions to the statute? If so, shouldn't that trigger the *Smith* exception for the unemployment cases, and bring into play not a requirement of respectful consideration but the Sherbert v. Verner requirement that the state's interest be "compelling"? Alternatively, does the Commission's refusal show that the statute does not authorize exemptions but merely does not extend to refusals to provide service based on the business owner's judgments about derogatoriness, that is, refusals based on some ground not protected under the statute?